Electric Earth

Electric Earth

✦

...a motor overheating

Will Jansen

iUniverse, Inc.

New York Lincoln Shanghai

Electric Earth
...a motor overheating

iUniverse books may be ordered through booksellers or by contacting:

iUniverse
2021 Pine Lake Road, Suite 100
Lincoln, NE 68512
www.iuniverse.com
1-800-Authors (1-800-288-4677)

ISBN-13: 978-0-595-38035-0 (pbk)
ISBN-13: 978-0-595-82405-2 (ebk)
ISBN-10: 0-595-38035-2 (pbk)
ISBN-10: 0-595-82405-6 (ebk)

Printed in the United States of America

Contents

This land that I traveled
Once fashioned with beauty
Now stands with scars on her face

The wide open spaces
Are closing in quickly
With the weight of the whole human race

And its not that I blame them
For claiming her bounty
I just wish that they'd taken her slow

—From a song by Willie Nelson—

PART I
The Problems

1

Global Wobble

There are many explanations being given to us by the scientific community of the world as to why we are suddenly, in the past 50 years or so, experiencing such a dramatic increase in natural disasters. We are told that these increases in earthquakes, volcanic eruptions, hurricanes and tornadoes, along with rising sea levels and melting polar icecaps, are probably the result of global warming. This is true to a certain degree but it is not the root cause. We are told that this phenomenon of global warming is just a normal cycle that the earth goes thru every so often. We are also told that there is nothing to worry about nor is there anything we can do about it other than to reduce the amount of pollutants we put in the air.

This is a very dangerous attitude for us to take because what is happening is not part of a naturally recurring cycle. Hydrocarbons and other pollutants that we add to the atmosphere are a part of the problem but they are not the main one. What we are seeing today has never happened before in the history of the world. Never before have there been so many of us, so efficient at what we do, that we are dramatically modifying this planets surface and affecting how it turns on its axis and interacts with the surrounding atmosphere. Because science, like medicine, has become so segmented, very few, if any of the practitioners have the luxury of studying the world as one complete system. They unfortunately must focus their energies on a narrow and particular branch of science in order to compete for grants, or to be of use to a company or a government that will pay for their services.

One of the problems this never before seen "Super Civilization" we are all a part of, is the many fold increase in the wobble of the earth called "Chandlers wobble". It should be pointed out that when a ball "wobbles" as it turns, it makes things on the surface of that ball, shake. In the case of this ball called earth, when it shakes, things like the tectonic plates which "float" on its surface, move. When these tectonic plates move, we get earthquakes. These plates only have to move a few feet to cause an earthquake and in relation to their size of thousands of miles across, that is not much at all. It is understandable that we do not personally notice this wobble because of our size as human beings in relation to the size of the earth. We just do not have enough mass in our bodies to feel the shaking or wobble just as we do not notice the speed we are turning at which is about 1000 miles per hour. Another speed we may not be aware of is the 70,000 miles per hour we travel in our orbit around the sun. When something as big as a tectonic plate is caused to move by a wobble like force acting on it, it will bump into other plates near it and the result is an earthquake or a volcanic eruption. These global disturbances, amongst others, are the result of how we have dramatically changed the relatively small part of the terra firma that we occupy on this planet.

Most of us live and build our cities in the northern hemisphere of this rotating world because that is where most of the less than 30 percent of the world's land is located. Inhospitable climates and terrain allow us to use only about 15 percent of all the land there is, which amounts to only about 5 percent of the surface of the world. I point out this seemingly inconsequential fact because when weight is taken from many places on a spinning ball and concentrated to only a few, imbalance results.

Before we showed up on this planet a few million years ago, more or less, the earth had plenty of time, a few billion years or so, to find the best way for it to go around the sun so that it could have nice seasons for things to grow on its surface, things that we human beings could get along with. Each little correction it made to its course around the sun took a long time to see if that correction was beneficial. It had to wait centuries, perhaps hundreds of centuries each time, for climates to settle down and for plants and animals on its surface to either thrive or become extinct. In some cases the earth found out that certain life forms that developed would not be compatible with human beings, so it made further corrections to its course. Dinosaurs certainly weren't compatible with us so it had to make them disappear by another course change. In conjunction with finding the most beneficial course around the sun in terms of climate, the earth also had to determine its best orbit in terms of the sun's gravity. Too close to the sun and we head into it. Too far and we go away from it.

This is not meant to imply that the earth "thinks" like we do and just "decides" to make the corrections she needs, but rather that this planet is a part of a natural system and just as a tree knows naturally to send its roots downward and its leaf bearing limbs upward, the earth knows what it must do to make this a livable place for us human beings. We are the noble beings of this world, installed here as caretakers. We are the only creatures ever here with the awareness and the ability to make choices in how we live our life and consequently, are the only ones capable of interfering with the way the world works.

There are many complicated mechanisms that need to be accounted for which is why it took so long for the earth to get ready for us. It also had to figure out just how fast to turn on its axis so that those things on its surface wouldn't fly off as a result of its own centrifugal force caused by its rotation. Things like us. It created oceans and mountains and moved land to wherever it needed it so that it could rotate without shaking. Volcanoes were activated to bring the weight of land from below where needed. It kept moving things around until its balance was perfect. In other words, it created a place for us to thrive because in its own way, in its own natural way, it knew that we were coming to occupy her, and things had to be just right so that we could create an ever advancing civilization which is our job on this planet. What this sentient being known as Planet Earth, didn't know, is that we would get to be so good at what we do, that we would start creating problems for her, and at the same time, for ourselves.

When we build the cities of the world and their corresponding infrastructures today, we do so much more of it and do it so much faster than any other civilization before us. The tremendous amounts of the various materials needed for our modern cities are now being mined or otherwise removed from the earth in one place and then transported to another place around the world. This is the main reason for the existence of our modern transportation systems. It is why we have so many trucks, railroads, ships and planes operating around the world all the time. Some of these are for transporting us, our food and other comfort items but the majority of our transportation systems are used to move construction materials to build the cities around the world to accommodate the ever growing populations of the world.

Combine the unimaginable weight of all these various building materials with the complete removal and, as a balancing factor in earth's rotation, other weight, in the form of hydrocarbons, (oil and coal) chemicals, minerals, gases and water and you can see that the weight of theses elements when added up, will amount to a very significant and almost incalculable number. Other weight changes we make to our planets surface are those done by building dams and changing the course of rivers, creating large inland lakes where they did not exist before.

If it seems at first glance, to be impossible for us tiny human beings to actually cause an imbalance in the earth's rotation on its axis, consider that a wheel, a rotating wheel like the tire on your car turns at only 60 miles per hour. This wheel can have its balance greatly affected by only a relatively small piece of lead weight added moved or removed. This earth turns at 1000 miles per hour and is actually a finely balanced very fast moving wheel acting as a gyroscope in its obit around the sun. Because of centrifugal force, the faster a wheel or globe turns the less weight you need to move around on its surface to affect its balance. In baseball, spitballs were made illegal because a tiny bit of spit on one part of the ball caused it to wobble and made it hard to hit.

This global weight redistribution around the world has been increasing at an exponential rate during the last few decades, right along with, and in most cases, exceeding the exponential growth of the world's population. Research into this practically incalculable and presently unknown massive amount of weight being removed or moved around on the earth's surface shows no evidence that the subject is even being investigated by scientific communities. Because "global weight redistribution" is not being considered as a factor in the alarming increase of "Chandlers Wobble" and resulting earthquakes and other geological disturbances, does not mean it isn't a factor, it just means that nobody is looking into it. Does anybody know what New York City Weighs? How about Tokyo, Shanghai, Sao Paolo or London? What about Lake Mead or just one shopping mall, parking lot, street or interstate highway? How much oil, coal, gas, minerals or water do we take out of the earth each day? What number would we end up with if we added up what we've used or moved during the past 50 years? Oil and coal alone is a very big weight number which is used up and the remnants dispersed around the world via the atmosphere eliminating it as a part of the earths balance scheme.

An example of this lack of consideration of global weight removal and redistribution is the work being done by some scientists dealing with the melting polar ice caps. Much effort goes into figuring out how fast they are melting; how the addition of fresh water into the saltwater is changing the way the world's undersea ocean currents run and how much the sea levels are rising around the world.

This is undoubtedly a very important field of research and needs to be understood but there is another component of all this ice being changed into water that also needs looking into. How much does all this water, that is being dispersed into the oceans of the world weigh? If there is a sufficient volume of water being added to the oceans of the world by melting polar icecaps that can raise the height of these same oceans numbers of feet, enough to flood many of our coastal cities, what about the weight of all this water being removed from the poles? While at the poles as ice, it obviously acted as part of the earths balancing scheme. This same melted ice, which represented weight at the poles, is being spread out amongst the oceans of the world and no longer acts as a balancing weight. It appears that in today's society, the only time weight is seriously considered is when we look in a mirror.

This author is not a scientist but rather, an interested observer unfettered by the unavoidable conventions of current scientific learning that make it very difficult to think outside the "conventional" boxes modern science has created. A lifetime traveling the world with a bird's eye view of this world from the cockpit of airplanes, has allowed me to glean certain uncommon and apparently unnoticed aspects of the changing surface of this world in the past 50 years. My purpose here is not to criticize the many wonderful efforts of science but rather to point out things that need further investigative effort by qualified people, to determine the value of what I say in this book. When they begin to see the patterns that exist, connecting modern construction and corresponding deforestation to so called "natural disasters", we can then begin to ask different questions and do something about what is happening around us. Perhaps it is time to develop a grid of the earth showing where weight is beneficial or not beneficial to the earth's rotational balance so builders can become aware of any impact they may unknowingly cause. This of course is a major undertaking and would require a whole new discipline of scientists. Maybe we could call them "spin doctors". On second thought, that name wouldn't work as we already have them.

It would be of more service to the world today if we looked into new ideas about how this world works and why it is undergoing such drastic and phenomenal change. Figuring out why we are suddenly experiencing so many "natural disasters" is much more important than knowing what happened millions of years ago, how the cave man lived, or how to make bombs to kill cities at a time or even to find out what other planets are made of. We have more pressing matters to attend to and this is where science should be using their considerable investigative powers. This is our home, our only home and since we are the only caretakers of this home, it behooves us to understand it more fully as a complete system. We need to understand its workings so that we can correct any wrong doings we may unknowingly be doing. As for facts concerning the increases in the earths wobble lately, one only needs to do an internet search on "chandlers wobble" and dozens, even hundreds of proofs are offered by many people, including well known scientists and various government agencies that study this obvious symptom of a world in trouble. This earth is wobbling more now than ever before and this same increase closely parallels the changes we have made to the earth in our immediate past.

2

Global Friction

The preceding dealt with a known condition of a wobbling earth. Straightforward logic was used to connect "Chandlers wobble" to the rise in earthquakes and volcanic eruptions by tectonic plates being moved around by this shaking effect as the world wobbles around on its axis more and more each year. There is another aspect of the earth's rotation that is overlooked. It has to do with friction between the earth and its atmosphere as it turns in its daily rotation.

Were you to be asked if you thought that the earth were in space, the answer would invariably be, of course the earth is in space, where else could it be? We have all been taught that this is so and now we even have pictures taken from space to prove it.

Sometimes what we see at first glance is not really what it appears to be. When we look closely at those pretty pictures of a tan, blue and white earth traveling in space, we can begin to realize that it is not just earth we are seeing but the surrounding atmosphere made up of mostly nitrogen, some oxygen and a little bit of other gases. These pretty looking clouds and invisible air are not attached to the earth in any fixed way. They form a completely sealed and separate environment around us, so therefore saying that the earth is in space, is not a correct statement. To be precise we should say that our atmosphere is in space but the earth is inside this atmosphere and therefore, not in space. If the earth were in space, we wouldn't be here. One could say that the moon is in space because it has no atmosphere.

This is not just semantics; saying the earth is in space is a very misleading way to see the world, a way that has been accepted as gospel since we figured out that the world was round and that we were a part of a larger solar system. When we collectively agree on something that in fact, may not be true, we run the risk of not being able to analyze further, those things that affect our lives and how we live them. When Columbus set out to find India, he ended up proving the world was indeed, a globe, and not flat, which was different from the collective thinking of the rest of the world at that time, he changed peoples thinking about the world and consequentially was a catalyst in many discoveries made since then.

The reason I bring up what may seem to some, an unimportant observation, is because the fact that the world turns inside its atmosphere of gases which we call air, and is not in space, is what leads us to the knowledge that this world is in fact, an electric motor. To be more precise, the world is a battery operated, rechargeable, electric motor.

There are some scientists that have done computer modeling of the interior of the earth that has shown the earth may be a motor of sorts. They used computers because it is obvious that we cannot know for sure what is way down inside this globe. So far we haven't gotten more than 7 or 8 miles deep into the surface of our planet, which is a long way from the 4000 miles needed to reach its center. In essence, we haven't gotten thru the skin of the apple yet.

A theory was developed by the use of computer models that there is an inner core of solid iron about the size of our moon contained in an outer core of moving molten metals underneath the mantel of the earth. This metal is an electrical conductor moving around the inner core exerting a magnetic force that causes this moon sized inner core to turn, which in turn, turns the world. They also say that this electrical energy flowing in the conductive molten metal was possible because there was a pre-existing magnetic field that formed when the earth was being formed. This was decided because we know that in order to induce a current of electricity to flow in a conductor, even a conductor like molten metal, a magnetic field has to be there.

If these same scientist's took their work just a little bit further they would have begun to realize, that, an electrical motor the size of earth, would require constant and massive new inputs of electricity in order to keep the motor running. Any motor needs to be able to replenish the energy that it uses. They should have begun to ask the important question, "where does all this electricity come from"? instead of deciding it was self sustaining. By following this thread of inquiry, they would have undoubtedly ended up with what is described in the following passages.

When we have a thunderstorm passing thru our area, we are both afraid and at the same time mystified by what we know as lightning. We know what to call it when we see it, but in reality, we know very little about it other than it is electricity in a very powerful form. Sure, we have measured how many millions of volts one bolt can produce and how it travels from cloud to cloud, cloud to the ground or vice versa, but we don't know exactly what causes it.

Many organizations and people study in detail the phenomena of lightning, including some like NASA (National Aeronautics and Space Administration) and NOAA (National Oceanic and Atmospheric Agency). When asked what causes lightning, the answer given by these venerable organizations is in effect that atoms in clouds collide and cause a build up of static electricity. They also admit that they are not completely sure just what causes lightning. This explanation seems a plausible one because we all know that static electricity can build up on us as we walk across a carpet and discharge as a spark when we reach for a metal doorknob.

When trying to understand lightning, it would be of help to remember that God, or Mother Nature if you prefer, never does anything just for fun. Everything that we see in this world and many that we cannot see have a purpose in the operation of the world and must be efficient. If something does not meet these basic criteria for being, it will eventually cease to be. I didn't make that up; it's a basic law of nature. If we would take more notice of that principle, we would have long ago begun to answer what should be the first mystery of lightning, which is why we even have it at all.

The question before science about lightning, has always been how we have it and has not yet pondered the why, much less answered the how. For something that occurs over 100 times a second every second of every day, somewhere in the world, I am surprised that there hasn't been investigation as to why we have this powerful display flashing all over all of the time.. Then again, I am not surprised because when something is around us all our lives, we tend not to question why its around, we may ask how it got there, but usually, not why, especially when we see it only on a local level as we would when a thunderstorm passes by. It's a bit like how we study the evolution of man, we want to know when we got here and how we got here but expend little effort to discover why we got here.

Relying on the law that everything in nature has a purpose leads us to understand that lightning is the energy created specifically so that this electric earth of ours can keep on turning at just the right speed around its axis. It is the lightning going into the ground and passing thru to the center that is constantly recharging the battery needed to supply electricity to create the magnetic field that exerts the force that turns the core of iron that in turn, turns the world. This is the real reason for lightning, not just to provide us with a beautiful light show on a warm summers evening or to add a bit of nitrogen to the soil. Nature would not spend her energy just to scare the dickens out of us with a bright flash followed by a loud noise. Her aim is to be always purposeful and efficient.

Isaac Asimov, a renowned cosmologist and physicist wrote a book that I read many years ago, in where he stated that in the very center of the earth there is a fluid that is so dense due to gravity's compounding effect, that a spoonful would weigh as much as a mountain. He called this fluid an "electronic fluid". I have always remembered that phrase and always wondered what would be the use of such a fluid if in fact such a thing did exist. I don't know for sure if it does exist and nobody else does either. However, it does fit the puzzle of how the world works and tells us that such a material would serve as an extremely efficient battery well suited to the world's electrical circuit. A battery that is constantly being recharged by the lightning being produced by the world's atmosphere to keep the world turning at the constant speed it must turn at. This, in effect, is what makes this planet of ours; a battery operated, rechargeable, electric motor. It is the biggest motor in the world because it is the world.

This idea that I am proposing of lightning being the energy source to turn the world is only valid if it can answer another question of why. Why does the earth need to be an electric motor? This is why I took your time and mine to discuss why it is important to understand that the earth is not in space. When we can agree that the earth is not in space, another very important piece of the puzzle of how the world works becomes apparent. Because the earth turns inside its atmosphere, the turning encounters resistance. This is something we cannot get around. This world of ours has to obey the same laws of physics that we do. Air has a certain resistance to anything moving thru it that has mass. We know this, airplanes know this and so do birds. Anything that moves against a resistance must have a power source to continue moving which is why the idea of the earth being a motor makes sense.

A body moving thru space will continue moving without a power source as we know from the satellites we put up to travel in space. It is true that this earth can continue its orbit around the sun indefinitely but that is because the atmosphere outside the earth is in space and therefore its orbital movement around the sun, encounters no resistance. The other movement of the earth, its rotational movement, does have resistance.

We all know that fish have scales, birds have feathers and some of us even know that sharks have little bumps on their skin which is why it feels like sandpaper. When we accept things we see all the time without question or at least a curiosity simply because they were always there, we lose an opportunity to discover more about our world than is readily apparent. Have you ever asked why a fish has scales? Sure they help protect a fish from other fish and the environment but why these little, slightly curved, scales? Why not a nice tough skin like on an eel?

How about the feathers on birds? Why so many complicated and delicate features? Sure it's obvious that they have to be lightweight and a feather certainly is that. The same effect could have been accomplished with a nice lightweight fur of some sort that would also serve the needed requirement of shaping it into a bulk of the right size and shape for aerodynamic purposes. We know that nature can do anything it needs to but why these particular scales and feathers and the abrasive skin of sharks?

The answer is because of a law of physics known as "Bernoulli's Principle". When Mr. Bernoulli formed his principle, I doubt that he knew how important its operation is to the world as a whole.

Bernoulli's Principle states that if you increase the speed of a gas or a liquid, you lower the pressure in that gas or liquid. This is the reason we are able to make airplanes fly. We curve the top of the wings so that air going over the wings, has to travel faster than the air going under the wings making the air travel further in the same amount of time. It's a well know principle that we take advantage of in many ways. In plumbing systems we reduce the size of a section of pipe causing the fluid inside to speed up and lower the pressure in that area should it be required, or we can make a carburetor suck fuel from a gas tank by causing the air to speed up as it goes thru a restriction called a venturi in the carburetor.

Nature uses this principle in more ways than we can imagine. As air flows around each feather on a bird, the pressure near that feather lowers because the air has to travel further around that slightly curved little feather and therefore has to speed up to keep up with the rest of the air it is flying thru. This lower pressure means that there is less resistance to the air near that feather because a lower pressure is in reality less atoms of air at that point. Less atoms to rub against that feather lets it move thru the air more efficiently. The same effect is produced as water flows around the scales of a fish and the little bumps on a shark, less water molecules to impede the movement thru the water. Sure it's only a tiny difference in each feather, scale or bump but add up the many little feathers, scales or bumps and you have a more efficient movement than you would if the animal were smooth.

In aviation, we call this the boundary layer, in computer talk it would be the interface. On a smooth surface, atoms tend to stick more than when the surface is somewhat irregular. A very simple example of this would be how your finger tends to stick more when you rub it across a piece of glass, compared to sticking less, when you rub it across the irregular surface of a piece of wood. Now I finally come to the earth's lubrication system.

Every forest, jungle, tree, branch, bush, leaf, or blade of grass on this earth has a purpose other than to feed us, or to make things look nice. They are here for the same reason that birds have feathers, fish have scales and sharks have little bumps. As the earth turns thru its atmosphere from west to east it encounters the resistance of the atmosphere that it must turn thru. If the earth were a smooth globe it would have to work harder and use more energy to maintain its required speed of one revolution a day. When nature finds a way that works more efficiently, she will use that method wherever possible. Nature uses "Bernoulli's Principle" with fish and birds and she also uses it to help the world turn. It's probably accurate to say that nature thought of it before Bernoulli did.

When I say that the earth has a lubrication system, I am talking about the various forms of greenery on our planet. All the vegetation covering the world is nature's way of allowing the planet to turn thru the surrounding and resisting air more easily. Every atom of air has to go around every piece of the vegetable kingdom that gets in its way. This makes each atom of air speed up in relation to other atoms not required to go around anything in their way. These atoms that are speeding up are putting more room in between each other compared to the other atoms that don't have to speed up. More room between each accelerating atom means more space; more space of course leads to less resistance.

This seemingly preposterous idea, that the green stuff of the world serves a purpose other than to feed us and the other creatures of the world, build stuff with, turn carbon dioxide into oxygen or to look nice should be judged as part of a whole. We need to keep in mind that everything we see in this world and even things we cannot see is made up of individual atoms. How each of these individuals behaves and how they interact with each other determines how the world is. It should be looked at as another piece of the great puzzle of the world that we haven't noticed yet because it's always been there, hidden in plain sight. The oceans of the world, also contribute to a more efficient turning of the earth thru the atmosphere with waves of the right size and shape.

At this point in the discussion, assuming you agree or are at least curious, it may become obvious that if we remove some of this "lubrication" in the form of greenery from the surface, it will become harder for the earth to turn in proportion to how much we remove. This is obviously a part of the reason why we are experiencing a warming of the earth. How much a part is yet to be determined. We have removed a very large portion of this greenery by what we call deforestation and progress. Even the worlds farmlands have been changed to a lesser degree of efficiency by "clearing" them of their original growth. It is said that not too long ago, a squirrel could go from one side of the United States to the other without touching the ground. Today, that squirrel would be lucky just to make it across the street. This removing of green stuff from the earth's surface is but one of many things we humans do without fully understanding the consequences of our actions.

When a motor has to expend more energy to maintain a certain speed because of added load or reduced lubrication, something happens, it heats up. Any motor does. In the case of this earth/motor, we have done things that not only reduce its natural lubrication but we have also done things that add to its load, such as a wobble or increased drag. In other words, we have become double trouble to this earth trying so hard to keep up its so necessary speed of rotating exactly once a day. One indication of a world trying harder is the fact that it is slowing down. It is a very slight slowdown but in something as complicated as this earth, even a very small change can have disastrous effects.

The addition of the many structures in the form of cities to the earth's surface lately has also had an effect on the turning besides the one of weight previously discussed. There is an economy of size and shape involved with Bernoulli's Principal. Trees and bushes are of the right size and shape to be of help. Square and tall buildings are not. Too many of these misshapen structures sticking into the atmosphere become what we know in aviation circles as drag. Natural features like mountains are here to help balance the world as needed in terms of weight and also to provide climatic differences but they are also shaped so they won't become a hindrance or a drag to the world's rotation. Isn't it amazing how Nature has figured all this out?

3

Lightning Production

Earlier I spoke of lightning and gave reasons why we have to have it as an energy source to charge the earth's battery. I also described the scientific community's latest efforts to explain how it is produced by atoms crashing into each other creating static electricity. Sorry, but that is not an acceptable answer because we certainly know how to produce electricity. We do it all the time

We move a conductor like a wire thru a magnetic field created by magnets and cause a current of electricity to flow in that wire. Atomic power plants do it the same way except they use steam from the heat of atomic reaction to turn generators which consist of wires turning thru the field of magnets or vice versa. The alternator in your car does it basically the same way. We can then conclude that in order to produce electricity all one needs is a conductor, a magnet and some movement. Guess what? The earth does it this way too. I'm again surprised that the scientific community, NASA or NOAA hasn't come to that conclusion. The earth has a built in method to produce all the electricity it needs. This is how she does it.

The earth uses conductors in the form of water bearing clouds like thunderstorms. (Water is a conductor of electricity which is why we don't put an electrical outlet near the shower.) It also has the magnet. The earth is one giant magnet. The magnetic field of the earth runs north and south. The winds of the earth move west to east. This is the perfect setup to produce electricity. Move the conductor in the form of clouds containing water across the magnetic lines of force of the earth and viola! We have electricity in the form of lightning.

This should have been obvious to those that study lightning but alas, unless you look for why something exists in conjunction with how it exists, answers are not so obvious. Another piece of the puzzle about how the world works is the fact that lightning strikes worldwide, has been increasing along with storms that produce this lightning. This is the earth's way of producing more electricity to overcome the added friction we create by deforestation and the added drag of construction.

While watching a program called "Center of the earth" on the Discovery Channel on TV, scientists studying the earth's magnetic field and its relationship to the iron core and its function as a dynamo to turn the earth, questioned how the magnetic field was maintained. If they could see that lightning was a part of this mechanism to keep the world turning, they would know that this is how the magnetic field of the earth is produced. The two elements, magnetism and electricity are mutually inclusive. Albert Einstein once stated that how the magnetic field of the earth was produced was one of the great mysteries of physics yet to be discovered.

Gee whiz fellas, anybody looked at an ordinary electromagnet lately? Connect an electric supply to wires wrapped around a bar of iron and you get a magnetic field emanating from the ends of the bar. When you have lightning producing, moisture laden clouds, wrapped around the iron of the earth, you effectively have the same thing. In this case it's a round core instead of a bar. A magnetic field emanating from the ends of the earth with a wire made of water wrapped around it. All it needs is movement between the earth and the wire. The speed of the flow of clouds or wire, around the magnet is what determines how much electricity is sent to run the motor. We have become an added load because of what we do so therefore climates must change to keep up with us. The earth needs more storms to produce more electricity.

This is why the perfect rotation of the earth on its axis needs to be more fully understood as to its importance to the well being of the world. We need to question why it has to be perfect rather than dismiss a small imperfection. Doesn't perfect mean perfect? We are the only things here that aren't perfect and look at the world thru imperfect eyes so we tend to accept small imperfections as natural. From the world's point of view, no imperfection is acceptable. The proof is its perfect rotational speed over an unimaginable long period of time. It is only since we began modifying the surface so fast that it finds itself with a slight imperfection. We have a round ball that we live on and we pay no real attention to its slight wobble. Every time this ball wobbles means it is using energy taken out of the energy needed to rotate at the speed it must maintain. It's true that the world turns almost perfectly because we know it has only lost less than a second in the years we have been timing it. What's to worry? In percentages it would be near immeasurable.

The worry is that we forget to look at it from the earth's point of view. We need to ask why the earth has to be so perfect. Why has it been so perfect for so long? If we could begin to understand that the earth's perfect rotation speed is what keeps all things in order and any deviation to this speed can trigger automatic responses to create more energy. More energy that is needed to makeup that less than a second of speed it lost, energy in the form of electricity and also the energy of hurricanes and tornadoes. When I see a hurricane or tornado on TV it gives me the impression that the earth is sucking in energy and the vortex is its straw. When we work harder, we need to breathe deeper, it is how we get energy, we suck it in. Many complex dynamics are happening that we do not understand or are aware of but one thing earth has to do is the same thing we have to do. Obey the laws of physics. The earth knows much more about the laws of physics than we do, it makes the laws. One known law we both have to live with is, use more energy, create more heat. From the earth's point of view, a bit more heat is acceptable but a slowdown is not. To maintain a perfect course, a gyroscope has to maintain a perfect speed.

4

Hurricanes and Tornadoes

Now that we have a fair understanding of that increase the speed, lower the pressure thing, I would like to provide some different answers for why we are seeing such an increase in hurricanes and tornadoes. They also are the result of what we do as a Super Civilization.

According to The National Oceanic and Atmospheric Agency (NOAA) in their 14th Symposium on Global Change and Climate Variations, there were about 200 tornado events in the area of the United States known as "tornado alley" in the early 1950's when records were begun. By the early 1990's more than 1000 a year were being recorded. Now in the new millennium, we have more than 2000 a year including many in areas that has never seen them before. Nowadays, it is not unusual to see 20 or more tornadoes occur in one day. What else has changed about the earth besides the buildings we have added to the landscape since the 1950's?

Because I am now revising this book previously written in 2003 to take into account what is happening in the year 2005, I can report that the incidence of hurricanes has also broken all previous records. Not only are hurricanes more numerous, they are also forming closer to the East coast of the United States. Much of this is attributed to global warming which is primarily blamed on the pollutions we add to the atmosphere. While that is certainly a contributing factor, there are other reasons these destructive forces are occurring more and more. There is a more logical explanation for what is happening with our weather, specifically, hurricanes and tornados, besides pollutions and "cycles" that the earth supposedly may go thru occasionally. What is it that has changed to account for such dramatic increases? Again the answer lies in plain sight, on the surface of the earth.

So as not to appear repetitive by talking about that ole Bernoulli thing again, I will discuss this episode on hurricanes and tornadoes in another fashion to try and make it a bit different. However, bear in mind that Senor Bernoulli will still be guiding the principles.

A hurricane and a tornado have a common structure. They are both vortexes, but so is what you see when you flush your toilet. Of course, I won't dwell on that aspect of a vortex. Another type of vortex is what you see when you row a rowboat. As you pull the oars thru the water, you can see little whirlpools forming in back of the oars because as you move the oar, you are causing the water to increase its speed near the oar so that it can get around that oar fast enough to stay with its larger body of water surrounding it. A vortex is a spiral. Spirals are very common in nature; even our universe is composed of many spirals which we know as spiral galaxies.

I do not propose to know what nature thinks, but I would assume that she uses a vortex type of form because of its high efficiency. If we want to cause an atom, an atom of air for example, to move as fast as it can with the least amount of power consumed to move it, we can use a vortex. An atom of air or water is caused by gravity to spiral down into an ever tightening circle like in a vortex and two things happen, first its speed has to increase as it circles down into smaller and smaller circles because all the atoms starting out at the top need to get to the bottom at the same time as the other atoms starting with them at the top. If they didn't speed up, they would begin to pile up against each other at the bottom of the vortex. The second thing that happens is the pressure drops, which in turn helps them to go faster. It's like a win win situation if your goal is to move fast. The faster you go, the less resistance you have. Now we can see why nature sometimes uses this "principle" wherever she needs to move certain things. It may be helpful to your understanding if you consider that the only things that move to any degree on this earth are water and air. Electricity also moves but I will discuss that later to show a strange similarity between water, air and electricity.

If your question is; why does the pressure get lower when air or water move faster? The answer is that the space in between the atoms that make up air and water increases and when you have more space in between atoms you have less pressure. This is evidenced by the upper atmosphere which has fewer atoms per cubic centimeter than air at sea level and therefore offers less resistance to something moving thru it. Another way to say it is; there is more space between the atoms in the atmosphere high up than the atmosphere at sea level. When you get to pure space where there are no atoms, there is also no pressure and so, no resistance. What you end up with is the opposite of pressure; you have a vacuum which is what space is. There's nothing there. This being the case, we can say that this lower pressure like found on top of an airplane wing or the bottom of a tornado or hurricane can also be called a partial vacuum.

Ok, now we know that Nature has a very efficient tool to use if she wants to use a hurricane or tornado on the earth. We can ask why Nature would want to use these very destructive "tools" but we could get into a philosophical discussion about whether or not Nature's nature is to be violent, destructive and vindictive. The idea of this book is to show that because of what we, as human beings, do on this earth, we are the cause of these various so called "natural disasters", and I will take the position that Nature is doing these things as a defensive measure for herself and at the same time, a protective measure for us.

Mother Nature, or more specifically, earth, finds herself in a catch 22 situation. She is out of balance, has more friction and has to work harder to maintain the rotational speed she took so long to perfect. Because she has to work harder, she uses more energy in the form of lightning and her temperature is rising. She knows that this condition is bad for her as well as us, so she has to get things back to normal as quickly as she can.

Mother Nature has no way to call out to us like a regular mother would do, and say; Hey you guys, knock off all that craziness, you're screwing up the way I'm supposed to work! You're putting too many heavy cities in the wrong places, they're too tall and the wrong shape. And another thing, quit taking so much stuff out of me and destroying so much of my green stuff cause I need it to turn and stop making so many lakes where I don't want them. Sheeesh!, when are you kids gonna learn?

Since we can't be told directly what we need to do, we have to figure it out for ourselves before our collective mother decides to put her foot down even more than she is doing now. If we're smart, we will know that we can't fight her, she's just too big. She is in a catch 22 situation and will kill some of us to save some of us. She knows that we can't leave home so she will destroy whatever we do that does not conform to her ways. She has already started.

As I am writing this I am also watching the weather channel on TV to see what Hurricane Wilma in the Caribbean Ocean just south of Cuba is doing. I have already had to leave my location in South Florida to escape the ravages of Hurricanes Katrina and Rita. Wilma has already broken all records as the worst ever and that's why I need to keep an eye on her so that I know when to get out of Dodge since I make my home in a hurricane susceptible RV. As each season comes and goes, more records are broken with hurricanes and tornadoes. They are getting stronger and they are more numerous. As with the earthquakes, scientists are telling us that this is only a cycle and we just have to grin and bear it. It too will pass and things will get back to normal. Yeah right! That's what an ostrich says as he sticks his head in the sand. This is not normal and it won't pass unless we do something about it. What we can do about it is described in Part two of this book, but for the moment let's take a look at why it's happening now.

5

Vortex and Heat Generating Cities

A building, especially a tall building, is a vortex generator. Wind flows around these structures just like water flows around your rowboats oar, only on a much bigger scale. When we look at the United States as an example, we can see that we have many more structures, buildings, cities and other various things sticking up from the surface of the land. Most of this has appeared in only the past 50 years or so. Aside from my contention that the weight of all this construction has an effect on the rotational balance of the world, there is another problem with all this stuff we build, namely, tornadoes and hurricanes.

Both are a type of vortex that has some very dramatic and disastrous results we are becoming much too familiar with lately. Both need heat to form and a warming earth certainly helps in that regard. The other thing they require is for air to move in a fashion other than a straight line so it can begin forming into a circular pattern. When we put something in the way of wind we make it divert around or over whatever it is we put in its way. Of course, if that something isn't strong enough to divert this wind, it will just knock it out of the way but I will deal with structure strength later.

During hurricane Andrew in August of 1992 I had occasion to visit Homestead AFB in Florida. While traveling thru the area that morning I noticed many roofs of houses had been lifted straight up from the house leaving the rest of the house intact as though it were done by a crew of carpenters with a crane. Most houses in the United States where snow loads are not a problem are built with low pitch rooflines because it uses fewer materials and therefore is more economical. To the wind, a low pitch roof is similar to an aircraft wing. As the wind goes over the roof, a lower pressure is created and this partial vacuum lifts the roof straight up and is carried away. Either we learn to build roofs unlike airplane wings or we keep on replacing roofs.

As the world turns from west to east, it rubs the lower atmosphere and forces it to move in the same direction it is turning. This is why we have the wind flowing around the world generally from west to east at an average speed of roughly 10 miles an hour. It moves a bit faster than the earth turns because it's lighter and is constantly being "pushed" ahead of the earth. The air higher up, being less dense and having fewer atoms per cubic centimeter moves even faster because it has more "space" and therefore less resistance to its moving. That's why the winds aloft are generally stronger. Ok, enough about the atom stuff already.

This planet may be big but when we look back at our recent progress, one can see that size is inconsequential to what we are capable of doing. Anyone that has taken a drive across this country or visited places in other parts of the world they have not seen for 10 or 20 years cannot help but be amazed at what we have accomplished in just the recent past. Have you ever gone back to a small town you knew or where you grew up and the roads and buildings in town were unfamiliar? Did you find yourself needing a road map just to get around? It used to be that we would look up and be thrilled if we saw a building more than 20 or 30 stories high, today we barely notice them. Some of us have gone back 50 years later and were surprised at how much we have "accomplished." This is happening all over the world.

We have gotten past the point of doing things just to provide for our needs. Not too long ago an apartment or a small house and maybe a car were considered a mark of success or being a part of the good life. Today it could be thought of as someone living close to the poverty level. I am not lamenting the "good old days," rather, I am trying to point out how much more stuff one needs and wants just to be considered "normal" today. We now are at a very dangerous stage of our development as a species, where ego, greed and materialism have become a more powerful driving force than survival. It is true that we have built a few great cities and structures in the past. This was mainly because of the inflated ego of a relatively few leaders and kings who wanted immortality or because of religious beliefs, but what they did then is nothing compared to what we do today. Compared to us as builders, we make the ancients look like they were children playing with a set of Lincoln logs or toy blocks.

Today it is different. It is different because of the tremendous advances we have made in construction technology and associated transportation systems, knowledge in general and the very fact that there are so many more of us. Historians estimate that only a few thousand years ago there were about 10 million of us on this planet whereas today there are approximately 7 billion. Keep in mind that a billion is one thousand million. In the past if a king wanted to build a city, a monument or other large structure, it took a long time and there was plenty of room to do it in. Today this power is in the hands of anyone with an idea for a project and the ability to create the proper paperwork that shows a profit. Today we have so many more rich people able to fuel the building machine. If an individual decides he would like to have a skyscraper to satisfy his ego or greed, it can be done and done extremely fast. Just find some vacant space or knock down a smaller building and put a skyscraper in its place. The two or three years needed to do this are nothing compared to how long things took in the past. In the past, the earth had time to compensate for what we do; today she has very little time so she is forced to compensate faster which means more violently.

Mother Earth isn't dumb, she may not be smart in the same way we are but she's certainly smart enough to know that she has to make some adjustments for what she feels happening to her skin like surface. She feels a lot of stuff coagulating in spots that feel to her like some sort of rash or growth that is starting to itch. She doesn't have hands to reach out and scratch so she does the only other thing she can do, (besides earthquakes and volcanic eruptions) she uses strong winds to blow them away and hurricanes and tornadoes are the strongest winds around. These "tools" are like a broom that sweeps away these irritants we call cities. The more we irritate her, the more she will sweep away these irritants. The more buildings and structures of the wrong shapes and sizes that we build, sometimes in the wrong location, the more she will do something about it. She will survive so that we will survive, that's her job.

To some of you as well as to myself, there may appear to be a contradiction in the idea that it is the earth that uses so called "tools" to combat our doings. If we are the ones that are the cause of these natural disasters, then we are the ones using them against ourselves and not Mother Earth doing it. Earth has always had these happenings around to aid her in the establishment of a perfect way of orbiting and rotating. What they are is purely a result of cause and effect, a result of the laws of physics. They happen because something about the world makes them happen. Much of the time it is the natural topography that interacts with the normal wind flow patterns but sometimes, it is a cause and effect made by us, as is happening now. I suppose that we could say they are man made but in the larger sense, you could say that that too is natural because it is natural for man to make mistakes so that he can learn from them and hopefully not repeat them. I suppose it's just part of the growing up of the human species.

As stated before, tornado events in this country of the United States have increased many folds. The air curling up behind each building and skyscraper it goes around becomes a vortex and pressures in that area are lowered. When you multiply that local lowering of pressure by the many buildings we have built in that area in the past 50 years, aggregate lower pressures in an area already prone to tornadoes only serve to help a tornado form. One of the main ingredients in a tornado is low pressure. The only thing that has changed to account for tornado events going from 200 a year to over 2000 a year in such a short time is the addition of the countless cities and buildings and the associated changes to the surface that we have made. The parallel of construction and the rise of these events are just too evident. Another curious phenomenon that serves to support the contention that buildings can cause tornados is the fact that tornadoes are non existent in a hurricane while it is at sea. When this same hurricane comes ashore and meets up with a city, all of a sudden, tornadoes are spawned. The North American continent now has the most severe weather in the world which is a significant fact considering that it is has become the richest and fastest city building continent in the past 50 years.

Hurricanes, being another form of vortex, are also on the rise but in this case it is happening in a more dramatic fashion because of how much bigger and more destructive they are than tornadoes. There are a few interesting points I would like to make regarding hurricanes. Hurricanes used to form mainly off the coast of Africa and then work their way across the Atlantic Ocean near the equator where the prevailing winds called doldrums are not working against them. Now we find them also forming close to the eastern seaboard of the United States and in the Caribbean Ocean. Why is this so? What has changed to account for this shift of their birthing area?

The answer again lies in what we do. We have built these super cities with their many skyscrapers (a telling word) along the whole east coast of the North American continent. We have created a 2000 mile long stretch of what can be described as a giant wall of vortex generators. As the prevailing winds blow across from west to the east, they encounter this wall and the pressure of these winds drop as they flow into the Atlantic Ocean. These winds have to speed up wherever they meet these structures. The overall drop in pressure, when combined with the warmer waters of the Gulf Stream just offshore, means conditions for formation of hurricanes have just been improved.

At present, only the pollutions emitted into the air causing a greenhouse effect are considered as a cause of global warming. There is much more to what we do in our misguided efforts to progress with civilization, much more than meets the eye. Another important aspect of how we are improving conditions for hurricanes to form is the tremendous amount of heat we are adding to the atmosphere by the electricity we use and other fuels we burn in these cities and elsewhere in the world. Each watt of electrical power we consume or calorie of fuel we burn has one result that is unavoidable, heat! Every time we turn on a light bulb, an air conditioner, a computer, a TV or a radio, anything at all that uses electricity or other fuel, we are adding heat to the air flowing around that building or city. As I write this on my laptop computer I can feel enough heat emanating from it to make my lap uncomfortable and it uses very little electricity. What is the sum total of all this heat we are generating by using all the various electrical devices in all the cities, towns and villages combined with the output of other heat producers such as vehicles, airplanes, and even the heat retaining buildings and concrete surfaces we have added to the ground? Every time a switch is turned on in the world, more heat is added to the atmosphere that wasn't there before. This urban heat island effect means that cities can become their own ecosystem. This added heat was created by us and its cumulative effect should be considered as well as pollutions and the "greenhouse" effect. We of this world today, can and do create a lot more energy and resultant heat than we could just 50 years ago.

The two most important ingredients in a recipe to make a hurricane are low pressure and heat. We are now, more than ever before, providing those ingredients by the cities that we build. I cannot propose any of these statements as fact because I have no way of proving them but the proof should be self evident. As I previously stated, the purpose of this book is to put new ways of looking at a problem, in front of people that do have the means to examine them, and let them decide their validity. It is necessary that we look at and understand other ideas as to why so much is happening so fast. If it turns out that I am correct or even partly correct in my assumptions then it will become obvious that we need to seriously reconsider our methods of progress. At this time, all I can do is call it a duck because it looks like a duck and it walks like a duck. Maybe we just have too many oars in the water.

If we look around us we can see that everything keeps adjusting and changing itself to acquire the form and traits necessary for survival. We do it, animals do it, and trees do it. The earth does it too. Even mountains grow and subside to accommodate the needs of the earth and in turn the needs of the human race. Continents have split and moved to allow this spinning planet to add or remove weight wherever it deemed necessary to establish an equality of weight around the world. Rivers, seas and oceans were created and shifted according to its needs. Volcanoes were activated to correct for any changes in its equilibrium by creating new land where required. Earthquakes are what we feel when the earth has to shift land whenever and wherever it feels it needs it. Forests, jungles, bushes and deserts along with oceans, rivers, mountains and valleys are all part of the mechanisms needed for it to rotate efficiently as it turns thru the atmosphere. All of these things are going on simultaneously and orchestrated by a sentient being, an alive and perfectly programmed entity created for the sole purpose of making a smoothly functioning home for us.

Why does it seem strange that the DNA of all organisms on this planet is so closely related? DNA is essentially the same stuff in a human and a fly as well as a mouse. It has been discovered that most of our genes and most of those of any other organism have no purpose, no purpose that can be accounted for other than to reproduce themselves as genes. Some DNA is to give you a certain eye color, some to tell you how to grow hair and so on. However, most of it is just there, seemingly with nothing to do. Nature, in my humble opinion doesn't do things just for the hell of it. Everything I see or even the things I cannot see have some sort of part to play in this drama we call life.

Scientists tell us that there is a majority of everything's genes that are reproduced over and over without any apparent purpose. There must be a reason for these unaccounted for genes. DNA is after all, a plan, a plan of the future. We and everything else on this planet, including the planet itself are all part of the same plan. The 60 percent or more of the seemingly unused DNA that all organisms have is there for a reason. Nature wouldn't waste her time reproducing time and time again the major part of every organisms DNA if she didn't have a plan in mind. All this DNA which appear to have no purpose is in reality the background plan, or you could call it the master plan. It is the plan to steadily advance civilization and all things are a part of this plan. There is a prerequisite to this plan though; it needs to be followed in an orderly and balanced fashion. It appears that human being type organisms are the only ones not adhering to the plan.

. We are in charge of this world. We are able to choose our destiny. The earth has no choice but to do what it was made to do, unlike us it cannot allow mistakes without immediately correcting them. When it finds itself operating outside its given parameters it must take action to correct any improper acts made by others. If we continue our efforts in the fashion that we do now, the earth will accelerate its efforts to counteract us, without regard to us.

The earth and the things attached to it, or better said, the vegetable and mineral worlds do what they do as a natural instinct. They have no choice because their instructions come from a higher power which I call God but you can call it nature or whatever you like. They simply cannot disobey their orders. The nature of fire is to burn, the nature of water is to flow. The nature of the earth is to rotate and go around the sun in just the right way so that we human beings can thrive.

This planet has been programmed to become a comfortable place for human beings but it doesn't know what a human being is. It doesn't exist on the same plane or level that we do. A rock has no awareness of the life of a tree or a human being. A tree has no awareness of the life of a human being or a rock but they do know what they are supposed to do. We, on the other hand and animals to a lesser degree, are aware of rocks and trees and have choices. We can do as we like but we do not have the same clear cut instructions as the other domains.

We have the ability to change our minds and accordingly the surface of the earth and thereby its interaction with its covering of the atmosphere and how it rotates on its axis. We have the ability to move and remove large amounts of materials and weight on the surface of this planet. This ability has developed in an orderly and steady fashion since we have been here. However, in recent years our abilities to create and construct, move and remove have far exceeded our knowledge of our world and what we are doing to it. Today we can add cities with towering skyscrapers and the corresponding infrastructures to the surface of this finely balanced spinning ball in just a few years. We dam up rivers that create very large lakes. We remove large portions of the natural surface. We do this without giving thought as to how this might affect how the world turns. The earth is starting to show signs of difficulty in dealing with the things we are doing to it. We are at war with the world and our weapon of choice is construction.

We know lots of things about our world and even things about other worlds, but we don't seem to know the overall picture of how our world works. If we knew, then we would know for sure that in many respects, our world is not working exactly right. It is not well. It seems to have a slight rising fever and in order for us to find out why, we need to first understand what is causing it and then prescribe the right medicine. Slightly rising temperatures and sea levels are only harbingers of what is to come if we don't change how we change the world.

PART II
The Solutions

6

A Building Legacy

Early man has passed on to us a legacy, a way of thinking, that in order for something to be strong it must also be heavy. This ingrained mind set persists today even though we have evolved to be so called "modern man". I am not criticizing early man for this legacy because conditions during his time were entirely different than ours today. About the only materials he had available were dirt, stones and trees. Whatever he built was of course, extremely heavy, but at the time there was no reason to think it should be otherwise. As he developed knowledge about his construction needs and some basic tools he was able to reduce these materials to more manageable sizes and shapes and gradually became more efficient builders. This went on for many, many years until other materials were discovered and invented and the building business took a giant leap forward. Before you know it we had wagons with wheels and other helpful gadgets to move these things around and attach them to each other. We learned that wood floats and we were able to venture out onto the seas and meet and live with our neighbors. Some of these neighbors were only too happy to copy what they saw, so building methods and techniques were spread around the world. After all, why reinvent the wheel?

Along came the industrial age and we were making all sorts of things with various metals, cements, wood, glass and other materials and we were making them look better too. Motors were put into the wagons so more stuff could be moved around and in order to get more stuff moving faster, bigger wagons with bigger motors were introduced. We started making bigger and better everything, houses, buildings, cars, trucks, roads, bridges, railroads and various other ways to improve our life. Rarely did the idea of weight reduction enter into the process because everybody knew that if it was heavy, it was good, it was strong and it was safe and there were plenty of these materials to go around. About the only time weight was a problem was in mining, harvesting, moving, or assembling it. To solve that problem we just invented more powerful and larger machines and vehicles. The world was full of these materials just there for the taking along with other resources called coal and oil that energized these projects and made every-thing go much faster. At the time the per capita use of these resources wasn't much of a problem so why try to use less of these abundant materials? That is what you would have to do in order to make things lighter in weight. The only people who gave passing thought to how heavy everything was were those poor souls moving it from place to place and putting them together. The terms, popu-lation explosion and conservation weren't very popular back then either, it's the way things were at that time and should have been because there just weren't enough people in the world to consider these things a problem. In other words, if it isn't broke, don't fix it! One by-product of all this rapid expansion of technol-ogy was more of us. As we progressed into the twentieth century and beyond more and more of us started showing up and we needed more and more stuff.

We just happily increased our efforts in collecting these materials and produc-ing more stuff. We began moving and removing enormous quantities of materials in the form of minerals, hydrocarbons, gases, and just plain dirt. Villages and then cities began sprouting up all over the world without regard to the effects all these activities were having or were to have on our little blue marble spinning in space or to the many little creatures including ourselves that call it home.

During this time someone got the idea of traveling through the air and Voila! Airplanes were born. For the first time in history, lighter thoughts were being thunk. Alas, this new way of thinking was only because air travel required it for the successful building and operation of aircraft and had nothing to do with a concern for the health of the world, which is the reason for writing this book. Efficiency and the safety of the things we build are other reasons. To be entirely frank I should also mention that the possibility of personal reward in the event this book should ever get published and sell enough copies for that to happen is also a slight consideration.

Aviation is the first segment of our modern world that gave cause to man to consider ways to build using lighter materials and methods to put them together. My own early training and experience was in the field of aviation and later on in the field of ordinary construction as a carpenter, I earned my living by lugging around and putting into place a lot of heavy stuff. I was also able to try other ways to earn a living that were easier by using lightweight materials that were available. Because government regulations and red tape concerning large products such as housing are too expensive and difficult for one person without the finan-cial means to overcome, I am putting some of these ideas in book form in the hopes that it may spark some interest in others. Since I have told you a little about myself, I should also tell you that I am basically a lazy person so my motives for exploring lighter ways to build were and are somewhat selfish.

If we want to continue this seemingly inevitable growth of the human race and at the same time to ensure better, not worsening conditions for the newcomers then we have to use what we have left much more efficiently. Present thinking in mainly industrialized parts of the world is betting on conservation and less progress as the obvious answer to many of our problems and as a way to let the newbies share in the earth's resources. I agree with the conservation part even though I don't always separate my garbage, hug trees or do all the things so many good people are doing to conserve. I don't know if it helps much but sometimes I use a toothpick more than once.

I submit to you, the reader, that by changing the way we think about building things, that they needn't be heavy to be strong, that we can not only continue progress but we can accelerate progress, reduce the damage done to the environment and at the same time, use less of what is left of our resources. Big talk, you say, yes it is big talk, but it is so important to all of us and to our heirs that we talk big about something so big, the future of us all. Before you decide that the author is just another kook with some crazy theory and rush to the bookstore to get your money back, please try to humor me and continue reading a little further. Besides, don't you find it a drag to stand in the return line?

Thanks, ok, where were we? Oh yeah, saving the world. Would you agree that if we could build most of the larger things we use in our daily lives cheaper and better and use less material that it would be of benefit to the world? Notice that I said cheaper which means less expensive but does not mean to infer inferior. It just seems easier to say cheaper. By "larger things" I am talking about vehicles, buildings, infrastructures etc! I am saying we can build these things using existing materials and technologies and at the same time reduce in many if not all cases the energy and materials required for their production by half.

This may seem to be an unachievable goal but be assured I am quite serious and intend to prove it in the following chapters. If after you finish reading this book, you will agree at least in the possibility of what I say, I will be happy. If some of you feel it is more of a probability than a possibility then I will be even happier because I have succeeded to some degree, in changing the way you think about building stuff.

Almost 200 years ago, scientist's decided to give an atom, a specific weight. They knew that hydrogen was the lightest element we have so they assigned it an "atomic weight" of 1, and every other element was numbered according to hydrogen. Oxygen weighs 16 times as much as hydrogen so its atomic weight is

16; iron is 56, and so on. This is because hydrogen has 1 proton in its nucleus, oxygen has 16, and iron has 56 protons. For obvious reasons, a singular atom was never weighed on a scale. You can't pick up something to put it on a scale if you can't see it, especially if a pair of tweezers is billions of times (or something like that) bigger than the atom. A quantity of hydrogen was weighed on a scale and this weight was compared to an equal amount of oxygen. This became the measuring standard for the weight of atoms of all the elements, as it is today.

In my opinion, an error was made back then, an error, by calling it weight. It should have been called, attraction units, or something that better describes how an object reacts to gravity. Science today, refers to the force between an electron and the nucleus of an atom as an "electrical attraction" and to gravity as the "attraction" between the earth and objects near its surface. There are many attraction type forces, such as, magnetic and a rubbed comb attracting bits of paper. People too, have some of these qualities, but we won't count that as part of this discussion.

I say an error was made because there is no such thing as inherent weight to an object, other than the fact that we call it weight or the object feels heavy. In other words, we have all agreed that weight exists and because of this, it appears that it does. When an object goes out to space, what happens to the "inherent" weight? Does it just disappear from the object? It is true that it still has its mass but that is not the same thing as weight. It will still take the same effort to push it as it would if it were on the surface of the earth but it doesn't want to fall down which is the weight part of it. What happens is, it gets to a point where it is out of range of the earth's attraction. We arbitrarily assigned the term, weight to an atom, which converts to pounds or kilograms, instead of the amount of attraction the atoms or molecules of the object has to the earth. We mislabeled the attraction force, probably because weight was a given, well before the atom was discovered to be the basic building block and scales were always calibrated in pounds or grams.

By doing so we may have denied any budding scientists and other interested persons the opportunity to investigate the possibilities of manipulating, or at least understanding more fully, this force. A force that is inherent in the atom itself. We also know, or better—said, do not know for sure that an atom has any substance or matter for that matter. We only know that the atoms and molecules were weighed on a scale a couple hundred years ago. A scale calibrated in terms of weight rather than in attraction units, which better describes the interaction between gravity and an object. Science has operated on a theory, set down by other scientist's almost 200 years ago, a theory that has worked very well. In other words, if it isn't broke, don't fix it. Does the squeezing together, of the atoms, in a piece of steel, cause the electrons or particle waves as they are known today, to interfere with each others orbits, or energy levels? Is this what makes steel "heavy", the fact that they are closer together? We have learned that we can overcome gravity somewhat by causing air atoms to separate as we do with air going over an airplane's wings. I use the term "energy levels" in relation to atoms because the latest scientific thinking, called quantum physics, is that electrons previously thought to "orbit" around the nucleus of an atom are now considered to be "waves." The height of these waves determines the energy level of the atom, the higher the waves, the higher the energy level. The waves in the open ocean are higher than the waves in a bay because they have more room to wave. Is an atom with higher energy levels lighter? If so, then is an atom with lower energy levels heavier? Who knows what could have been accomplished during the past few hundred years if we looked at weight as something other than an inherent heaviness in objects themselves, rather than an inherent attraction force. I realize this doesn't make a difference as to how things act, but sometimes how we label something can make a difference. So as not to confuse the issue, I will continue to refer to attraction force as weight, for the purposes of this book.

Forgive me for bringing up Mr. Bernoulli again but I previously mentioned that I would show a curious relationship between water, air and electricity. That is, if you increase the speed of a gas or a fluid you decrease the pressure inside the gas or fluid.

The college aviation course I taught involved various subjects, physics, meteorology, and electricity, to name a few. In order to teach about electricity, it was necessary for me to study the subject rather intensely, because it is not one of my strong points. I still have trouble installing a 3-way light switch in a house I may be working on. While teaching the basic elements of a circuit and how current, called amperage, reacts to a resistor, a restriction to the flow of electricity, I found out that the voltage, which is the pressure of the flow, drops or is reduced at the point of the resistor. I thought, well now, isn't it strange that electricity acts in the same way that water and air act in this regard, when forced to go thru an area where it apparently must speed up, the pressure drops. I know that electricity travels at the speed of light and should be a constant but why does it have a pressure drop just like air and water? Is it possible that the atoms or electrons or waves, or the electricity itself is speeding up somewhat as it travels through the resistor or the pinch in the line? Is it speeding up just as the atoms do in air and water when going thru a restriction? Einstein was always looking for what he called a "unified field theory" or, what is the basic connection between things that make the world work? When we talk about work, we talk about movement and as far as the surface of the earth is concerned, air, water and electricity are the things that are actually moving to any degree, besides the earth itself. I know it seems strange to think that electricity has something in common with water and air but according to Ohm's law and Mr. Bernoulli, it does.

7

Lightweight Construction

In aviation, we use a "power to weight" ratio to describe the power of an engine compared to its weight. In construction we need to have a similar term that would describe the weight compared to the use of whatever it is we are building. A "weight to use" ratio would give us a measure of its efficiency. An example of this would be the weight of a house compared to the weight of the occupants and their belongings. Another would be, the weight of a car vs. the weight of the people using it.

The idea I am trying to convey is, how heavy does something really need to be to accomplish its task? Does the weight of a house really need to be a few hundred thousand pounds to shelter a few thousand pounds? Does a car really need to weigh several thousand pounds just to carry around a few hundred pounds of passengers or stuff on the average? A modern jet passenger airplane weighs about 300,000 pounds to carry about 40,000 pounds of people and their baggage. Granted, they need to be designed for their maximum use and performance but what if this could be done where the structure itself, the house, the car or airplane could be built weighing significantly less and still perform as well? If you could cut the weight by, say half, would it be more efficient? In the case of a house it would require less building materials and less labor to build it. Granted, it would need to be strong enough to do its job. A car would be more efficient if you could cut the weight by half because the car would need a much smaller and therefore a lighter motor and associated running gear to achieve the same performance as a car twice the weight.

The airplane benefits are readily apparent. I will discuss houses and airplanes in more detail later, including boats. As for a car, all parts of the car would be subject to less stress due to the reduced effects of inertia and that old bugaboo called gravity. The heavier something is, the harder it is for it to change direction. A bump is really a rather fast change in direction. Another performance issue that would be greatly improved would of course be that much less fuel and oil would be needed to operate the car at the same speeds as the heavier one. Multiply that by a zillion or so cars and see if it won't help with our pollution problems. OK, I know that zillion isn't really a number but it is descriptive, besides, I have no idea how many cars there are in the world. Also, you wouldn't need to carry around as much gas, which also has weight, to travel the same distances. Braking distances would be decreased and handling characteristics would be improved because the lighter something is the easier it is for it to stop or change direction.

As for driving on snow and ice, again, inertia enters the equation. A lighter car in the same conditions as a heavier one would want to slide less because it has less impetus or call it desire, to slide. Less wear and tear on the roads being traveled on is another benefit of lighter weight cars. These are some of the operational benefits that could be achieved by reducing the weight of the car not to mention safety which I will discuss later but for the moment know that lighter stuff hits with less force than heavier stuff.

I have noticed that the Government puts limits on how much mileage a car should get but they never seem to get to the crux of the problem, which of course, is the weight of the car. It's true that manufacturers are using more plastics, but cars do not seem to be getting much lighter. The auto industries answer to weight has always been to add more power in the form of a bigger engine and that again adds more weight and more fuel. This philosophy is a dangerous vicious circle. Why not put some restrictions on the weight of the car? Wouldn't this increase the mileage? When the producers know that they have to build their products lighter in order to put less of the pollutants in the air, they will figure out how to do it.

We have available today the materials and technology to accomplish this but because of our inherited way of thinking about building it just doesn't seem to be happening. Engineers and designers are not to blame because they are taught by other engineers and designers and they in turn were taught by other engineers and designers and so on. The emphasis has always been on speed, looks, comfort, and safety and I have no problem with this. What I do have a problem with is how this is accomplished. How can we possibly improve on our wonderful, modern, hi tech way of doing things?

The answer lies in developing ways and means that are relatively low tech and to use fewer parts. I do not include the makers of computers in this discussion, as they are one of the few industries that have successfully and dramatically reduced the weight of their products, they have done this by making them smaller, whereas, this book deals with big stuff, and how to make them as big, or even bigger, while at the same time making them lighter. I will show how this can be done as this book goes on but first lets look at some other benefits that would result by reducing the weight of a car. Basically, half the weight means half the energy would be used to build the car, half the raw materials are mined, half the transport of materials to the builder is necessary and half the pollution created by the building and use of this car is put into our world. Half the deaths and injuries associated with cars is also a very real possibility and that in turn would lead to half the insurance payments. When I say we could reduce all these things by half I do not mean exactly in half, some of these elements could be reduced by more than half and some by less. It is not possible to put an exact figure on such a broad array of possibilities but you get the idea.

Some will say that industry could do this today but they just don't want to. To do so would reduce the price of cars and the use of gasoline. I agree with the reduction in price and less use of gas but disagree that they could do it today because of how this industry thinks or more precisely, how they do not think.

My experience in construction has shown me that not only is weight not given enough weight as a consideration, lightweight construction is not even considered a field of study, it has scant academic standing and there are few groups of people collaborating on this topic as you would find in most other fields that are involved in some way with all of us. There is some interest in the field of lightweight construction (May I call it a field?) in Germany but other than that I find very little interest in something that has so much importance to so many of us. There are a few isolated pioneer companies producing lightweight housing components and others involved in racing boats and home built aircraft but not enough for it to become general knowledge or as a way to accomplish some of the tasks previously discussed. There are a few books available on the internet about this but they are mainly directed towards advanced engineering students and other professionals. No point in lamenting about this because if it were general knowledge I wouldn't be writing about this.

As I write, it comes to mind that there is one field or industry, that is very involved in building something that has excellent weight to use and serves as a very good example of what can be done and is being done not by engineers and designers, but by mainly young people. These people are "surfers", yes I said surfers. They have learned to use a technique called composite sandwich construction, and have reduced the weight of surfboards from around a hundred pounds to boards weighing in the teens that perform better than their predecessors. Actually, they help to prove my point because a surfboard has to support more than ten times its own weight, is subjected to extreme forces, and still is able to maintain its integrity, even in extreme conditions. Imagine the stress it must endure when a giant wave crashes down on it, twisting and turning it at high speeds and pressures, yet these boards do a remarkable job of surviving that kind of treatment.

The fact that it is so lightweight is one of the reasons it can withstand these forces because its inertia is at a minimum. A heavier board would not be able to change direction as easily or as quickly as a lighter one. In the raging turmoil of a breaking wave it must be able to do that or, itself, break.

A surfboard, for those not familiar, is made by encapsulating a rigid lightweight plastic foam in a thin plastic skin, usually a type of fiberglass or even a carbon fiber cloth impregnated with resins which are also a plastic. This forms a structure known as a composite or sandwich panel that has a remarkable quality called a high "strength to weight" ratio and is an example of a construction method that can replace the typical "frame" type method generally in use today to build most of our larger structures and vehicles, including aircraft.

Most of the things we build today use a method that is similar to the human body. We build a skeleton or frame and then cover it with various "skins" like wood, metals, cements, and plastics. In the case of houses we use metal or wood for the skeleton or frame and cover the frame with these various materials. In the case of large or tall buildings we use steel beams and girders for the frame and cover them or "skin" them also. In the case of airplanes we build the frame of ribs and stringers of aluminum and skin them with sheet aluminum. Cars also have a frame built of metal, mostly steel, and are skinned with steel or in some cases, partly with plastic.

Aside from those structures built from solid materials such as stone, concrete, cement blocks, bricks and timbers which are in a class all by themselves because of their extreme weight, most of the things we build today are similar to natures way of building, mainly, a frame inside and a skin outside. Animals, birds, most fish, even people are built this way. Please understand that I am not presuming to improve on nature's way of building, only on the way man does it. We have copied nature in a sense by using the example of skeleton and skin and it has worked very well for many years but because we need to build so many large things that use so much materials there is no way we can continue in this fashion without harming our fragile little blue marble more and more as time goes on.

Nature has ways of efficiently controlling and recycling everything it creates, we do not. We need to change or die. I don't mean individually or right away, I mean, die as a civilization or to be more direct, eventually as a species. Sooner or later we will run out of stuff to build stuff with or the residues of this stuff will become intolerable. We have to find better ways to build what we need that use less of our resources. I hate to use this following term because it sounds like a threat but it should be considered a warning............. Or else!

There is a way to build what we need by again copying nature's way. This involves another realm of nature that most of us don't like to think about, much less see. Insects! Yes, bugs! One thing these tiny critters are known for besides being pests is their amazing strength to weight ratio. Who hasn't seen an ant on a TV show carrying around something far bigger and heavier than itself? The main difference between those little critters and most of the bigger critters in terms of how they are built is that they have their skeleton or frame on the outside. It's called an exoskeleton. In that respect, the surfboard I mentioned is quite similar to the ant. Sorry, it's the best analogy I could think of.

Now, let's examine why this ant and this surfboard have a better strength to weight performance than if they were built like we are with a frame on the inside. Most insects have a skin that is stiff and hard, yet slightly flexible and separated by a lightweight material inside that is not very compressible. In the case of the ant it is mainly fluids and muscles inside and in the case of the surfboard it's a lightweight plastic. Both serve a same purpose, to keep the outside skins separated. When we think about construction materials, one of the first considerations is how strong it is and will it bend or break easily?

There are two main forces that act on let's say, a 2x8 floor beam or joist. It is spanning across a room along with others and they have plywood laying on them and nailed in place. When you walk into the middle of the room on top of the plywood you exert a force. One of these forces is compression, which is applied to the top part of the 2x8 and another is tension, which is exerted on the bottom of the 2x8. The top is being squeezed together and the bottom is being pulled apart. The 2x8 can withstand the compression better than it can withstand the tension because of the wide plywood sheet on top which is also compressed. If you invite a lot of friends who are rather large, to join you in the middle of the floor you may exert more pressure on the 2x8 than it can handle and the very bottom of the 2x8 will start to separate. As it separates the tear will travel up to the plywood on top and it too will go through the same process. The bottom of the plywood will come under tension and begin to separate until it too fails and before you know it you and your friends are on the floor below. Next time choose your friends more carefully or choose less of them.

However, if you insist on inviting these same friends again what you could do is nail another sheet of plywood underneath the 2 x 8's, just as there is on the top and then this floor will be much stronger. The floor will now be strong enough so you and your friends can party away and even dance if you want to. This is because the width of the bottom of a 2 x 8 is only about 1½ inches. (Calling a 2x8 a 1 ½ x 7 ½ would just confuse us carpenters) When you add the three other 2x8's under this sheet of plywood then the total width of wood on the bottom of the 2x8's under tension was about 6 inches. When you add another skin of plywood under the floor you now have an additional 48 inches of wood to resist the tension on the bottom. A composite sandwich panel uses the same principal, a skin on both sides and instead of the 2x8's in between there is a lightweight material of sufficient thickness and resistance to compression and shear to keep the two skins separated.

A lightweight core in between the skins of such a structure can increase the stiffness or strength proportional to the cube of the core. What this means is that you can build something much stronger simply by increasing the thickness and can do so without adding significant additional weight. In the example of the floor given above, using 2 x 8's, you could also increase the strength of the panel you created by using 2 x 10's or 2 x 12's but you would also be adding significant weight. It should also be noted that the frame type floor of 2x8's and plywood mentioned above has twice as many parts as a comparable sandwich type panel would have without even counting the nails or screws.

I apologize for the long diatribe in carpentry, physics and talking about bugs. I realize that many of you are very knowledgeable in these things but if this book is to be of any use I must try to help those that are not involved in the arts of construction to understand that it is possible to improve our methods of construction and in turn help ourselves by building things cheaper, quicker and better by building them lighter and last but not least by using less parts. Keep in mind that each part needs to be produced and put in place by someone, so that, if you use fewer parts, it takes less time to build whatever you're building.

8

Houses and Buildings

What is a house or a building? It is shelter, a shelter from weather. The shelters we build are probably, the worst examples of the comparison of weight to use that I can think of. One of the best places to use the advantages of lightweight construction is in a typical house. Frame houses, a brick house, a cement block house, all have many, many parts that add up to an awful lot of weight. They weigh many, many, thousands of pounds, to shelter a few thousand pounds of people and their stuff. Most of the strength of the structure is used to support the materials themselves that the house or building is made of. This is not necessary nor is it very economical.

The average price of a home in this country is well over $200,000 dollars. Granted, the land is a large part of the price, but I will speak to that problem a little later on. The main force that needs to be considered when building a house or a building is the weather and gravity. A structure needs to be able to withstand high winds. When we build a square house like we usually do, we invite winds to blow them down. A preferable shape would of course be round, because a round shape is much more resistant to winds force. If building in the conventional square manner, we should at least place wind deflectors to disrupt the flow over the low pitch roofs we build so they don't act like an airplane wing. Since hurricane Andrew, building codes have been changed to require adding "hurricane straps" to tie the roof to the frame of the house as a way of solving this problem. A typical 2000 square foot roof has more "wing area" than many commercial airplanes which can lift off the ground at speeds less than those generated by a hurricane. Adding straps may be a help but does not get to the root of the problem.

The building codes in this country just don't allow you to build according to your own knowledge. They make it too expensive in terms of paperwork, money and time for someone to even try it on an experimental basis. Maybe someday, they will allow it like they allow a person to build his own experimental airplane, which lets you build it as you want and fly it, but only for yourself. There should be a plan where you can build but are not allowed to sell, until a few years have passed and the structure has proven itself in use. Many innovators of all sorts of products find that it is easier to make what they have innovated, than to overcome the many obstacles put in their way by the powers that be. This is not sour grapes; it is a fact of life. Ok, maybe it is sour grapes.

Ok, back to the house and how to build it. Because a house has very many parts involved in its construction, one of the first considerations is to reduce the number of parts required, while at the same time use less expensive and less heavy materials. At the present time there are two building materials on the market that meet these requirements. One is cement and the other is lightweight plastic foam called, expanded poly-styrene, otherwise known as EPS. A 4 foot x 8 foot x 6 inch thick, EPS panel, coated with a relatively thin coat of fiber reinforced cement would be the basis for building a house that has the qualities needed. Its compressive strength is about 1400 pounds per square foot for the foam alone. A 6-inch thick square foot piece only weighs one half of a pound. It is strong, cheap, insulated, waterproof, fire resistant, lightweight and does not rot. Since this core material can be cut and shaped with only a hot wire, and cement can be sprayed or hand applied before or after it is in place, the actual construction process is extremely simple and non-labor intensive compared to typical frame or block construction. Plumbing pipes and electrical wires are routed thru simple grooves in the panel. Floors and roofs can have extra reinforcing added as needed in the form of steel wire mesh or other devices or simply made thicker.

The cost of such a house, because of the use of less parts and labor can be less than half of what it costs to build a conventional house. We could be doing this today, but for the government system that does not allow it. Actually it is being allowed in some places but not in very many unless one wants to spend all his time and money going thru batteries of testing and other red tape type paperwork. I should also mention the mindset that it has to be heavy to be strong. By now, you should have an idea of the basics of this type of construction, so in the case of buildings, I will only say that if it needs to be stronger or taller, make it thicker. Tall buildings can be built by making the lower walls thicker than the upper sections. Skins can be made of other materials besides cement. The problem with the extreme weight of the buildings presently constructed is the fact that all this weight always wants to come down. It is what is known as gravity.

The tragic event of the World Trade Center collapse is a result of the upper floors, above the area of impact, weighing so much that the floors below the damage could not support the weight of the upper floors once some of the steel beams failed. This was evident because it took some time for the beams to fail due to the heat generated by the aviation fuel. Had the buildings been lighter in weight, especially the upper floors, the secondary disaster of collapse would not have occurred. This is not Monday quarterbacking, it is a simple statement of fact and a basic rule of gravity. The heavier something is, the more it wants to come down. Most injuries and deaths in an earthquake are the result of something heavy falling down. Lighter weight structures can also survive earthquakes better because the heavier something is the more it wants to continue shaking once it has started and the more it shakes, the weaker it gets. Another benefit of the type of lightweight construction I am championing is the inherent flexibility of using a lightweight core. If a tree didn't flex a little in a strong wind it wouldn't be a tree for very long.

There are some areas of this country, where flooding is a major problem. The house stays where it is and the water rises inside. When the flood recedes, the damage is still there. Water soaked wood and electrical circuits, ruined sheetrock, rusted nails and metal, and various other water damages are the result. Replacing walls or floors or even parts of them gets to be pretty costly. If houses were made of materials that weren't affected by water and the house were allowed to "float" up, held in place by tethers or other methods, it would mean that after the waters subside and the house returned to its original position, life could go on as before. A slab, one foot thick, built of a lightweight core and a cement skin would be enough to let the entire house float up and then and return when the water receded. It's what I would call a "go with the flow" approach to building in flood areas. Incoming utility lines would need to be made flexible to allow for a few feet of upward movement but that can be easily accomplished. It isn't exactly rocket science to figure out that if the water rises, so should the house. Duh! After hurricane Katrina destroyed New Orleans and other cities near the Gulf of Mexico, I offered my expertise to government leaders in that area but was unable to generate interest. There are many ways to overcome many of the problems we have today but they require a change. I realize that change is difficult, but when it is a change for the better, the possibility should be looked at. A house is the biggest investment most of us make; shouldn't it be something that will last?

9

Cars

Cars could today be built today using similar techniques used to build those amazing surfboards. A core of rigid lightweight plastic foam, encapsulated in a skin of other types of plastics that have the ability to be sprayed or layered would be the basis of such a car. The entire body and floor would be produced in a mold with the finish already in place. Areas of the car could be adjusted in terms of thickness and toughness according to needs. For instance, the front and rear of the unit could be made thicker to allow for more shock absorbing qualities along with the doors and interior dashboard area. Seats can be molded as strong lightweight structures also. Floors could be designed to allow for any space required for the running gear such as transmissions, drive shafts, axles and wheels which could all be designed smaller and lighter to suit the reduced weight and use these parts would serve. Areas of attachment for these and other parts and accessories can have imbedded into the molded sections appropriate connection plates and devices. Any area can be further increased in strength simply by adding more of the exterior and or interior plastic skins or adjusting the density or thickness of the core material. Notice that I said, exterior and or interior skins, which are both contributing to the strength of the structure, whereas in today's typical frame construction only the exterior skin is used for strength while the interior is mainly for cosmetics or comfort.

Those parts of the car that are subject to impact, such as sides, front and rear could be additionally protected simply by making them thicker. This would be similar to putting air bags all over the car because as we all know; lightweight rigid foams of various types are used today for just that purpose. They protect products from damage during shipping. Areas where there may be high heat from the engine or exhaust could have appropriate heat resistant materials such as metal or ceramics set into the structure before the molding takes place. Because of the nature of the molding process and the removal of the part from the mold it would be necessary to make molds for several different sections of the car such as front, rear, top, bottom and sides or however the experts in making molds determine as this is a discipline all its own. It is an established fact that production by molding is a more efficient and precise way to manufacture.

Because this would be a new way of doing things for the auto industry, it would require a certain amount of research and development and learning, but the benefits would be enormous to the producer, to the user and to the world. It will take a person or groups of people with the foresight, vision and the courage to initiate this kind of change. It will also require financial investment but how much does the industry spend just in retooling for one new model? I am sure there are leaders in the auto industry that, once they understand the advantages of using these comparatively simple, yet effective technologies they would want to be the first to make use of them. To be the first to come out with a car that weighs half as much as the competition and performs as well or better would be quite an accomplishment. A car that is safer, a car that costs less to buy and to operate, a car that will put fewer emissions into our air both in production and in use. A car that can produce more profit for the maker because he can increase his margins and still sell it cheaper than the competition and sell more of them.

This can all be done but it will take someone to do it. If you are one of those persons that have the ability to change how we build cars, please be advised that my intent here is only to pique your curiosity and hopefully get you to at least look into the possibilities. You could end up doing yourself and the rest of us a very important service.

Until the day that all cars are made much lighter in weight, we will not achieve the greatly improved safety record that is possible. By driving a car on the road today that weighs half as much as other cars, you would not be any less safe than you are now because the improved handling and braking characteristics would help to keep you out of harms way. The idea of not having any hard stuff on the inside of the car that could harm you, along with the fact of less inertia and shock absorbing materials completely surrounding you when you hit something else, or when something else hits you, will be a saving grace.

The real improvement in highway safety statistics will become evident, as more and more cars are made lighter. What this means is that if the vehicle laws were changed to ensure a gradual lightening up of cars, we would see a corresponding improvement in the rate of deaths and injuries caused by accidents. The only way this can come about is for the governments to begin limiting the weight of cars or the manufacturers doing it voluntarily. If the government wants to help, than instead of requiring better mileage, they should concentrate on the weight of cars which is the real root of the problem. Most cars are off the road after about 10 years, so that in a relatively short time, we could all begin to enjoy the many benefits of weight reduction. The sooner we start, the sooner it can start to happen.

10

Boats and Ships

The building method I champion in this book, the method of a frameless, light-weight type of construction, is useful when building cars for the reasons I have described. It's even more useful when applied to houses and buildings for obvious reasons. There is one mode of transportation that we use where weight is accorded even less consideration in the planning of its construction, less than those mentioned above.

That mode of transportation is boats, or as they are called when they are bigger, ships. What is the primary purpose of a boat or a ship? It is to enable us, and our things, to travel on water without getting wet. Some boats allow us to travel more comfortably than other boats, some are faster than others and some are more safe than others but all have one thing in common, they all float. Or at least they do most of the time. Boats float because of their shape, just as airplane can fly because of the particular shape of their wings. A boat is shaped to take advantage of something called displacement. It pushes enough water out of the way until the water moved out of the way by the boat sitting in the water weighs as much as the whole boat does. Water weighs about 60 pounds a cubic foot so if the boat weighs a thousand pounds, all it needs to do in order to float is push away one thousand pounds or 16 cubic feet of water and it will float.

A one thousand pound boat can do this and still have most of the boat sticking out of the water. This is relatively easy to do because even a heavy cast iron bathtub can float. All it has to do is make a hole in the water big enough so that if that hole were filled with water, that same water would weigh a little more than the bathtub. This is one reason why boats are generally built heavy, it just isn't that tough to make them float so why bother try to make them light. And anyway, heavy is strong, everybody knows that. Of the three main methods of transportation, cars, planes and boats, a boat is the one that needs to be the strongest.

Why? Because a boat takes more of a beating in use than does a car or a plane.

Anyone that has cruised at even moderate speeds in a little chop in a boat has felt that foot jarring pounding coming up thru the floorboards each time the hull hits the next wave. A car has shock absorbers and tires to soften the bumps in its road and a plane travels on a road of air, which is a lot softer than water. A boat however, travels on a road that most of the time is not smooth, and the faster you go, the harder the bumps. It's true that some boats can rise above the small bumps to smooth out the ride by attaining a planing speed but the bow and hull will still take a beating as it hits the top of each wave and the faster you go, the harder the hit. If the space between the waves is more than the length of the boat and you go fast, you will ride up each wave, become airborne for a moment, and crash down the other side with a pretty good thump.

The heavier the boat is, the harder the thump. Drop a balloon on the floor and it will just bounce a little but drop that same balloon filled with water and it will break. Why does it break? It breaks because it was a heavier balloon. It hit with more force. It had more energy. Two boats, same size, same shape, same strength, one weighs 1000 pounds and one weighs 500 pounds. It is easy to see that the lighter boat will take less of a beating given the same circumstances.

Remember that part about displacement? Where the boat makes a hole in the water big enough, so that hole, if filled with water that weighs as much as the boat, the boat will float? OK, now you have a break or a leak in the boat and you start filling that hole in the water with water, only it's inside the boat. If the hole in the water gets too small you don't float. Now, if you build a boat where the structure itself, even if completely submerged, displaced enough water to equal its own weight, the boat would float. It would bob up again even if you pushed it completely under the water because the entire boat weighed less than the water it was displacing even by being under water. How do you do that? You make it thick. Thick enough, so that, the thickness of the hull by itself, displaces enough water that weighs enough, to equal the weight of the boat.

If you make the hull, say, a 2 inch thick hull, comprised of a rigid lightweight core which has a weight of one pound per cubic foot and a tough skin on both sides that weighed say one pound per square foot you would have a structure that weighs about one and one sixth pounds per 2 inch thick square foot. A, 2 inch thick, square foot of water weighs about 10 pounds, so even if you completely fill this boat with water it won't sink. You could blow the boat to pieces with dynamite and the pieces would still float. It would just refuse to sink. The reason a wood boat will sink even though wood itself floats is because a 2 inch thick square foot of wood weighs about 7 pounds which is less than the weight of water but, when you add in the weight of the motor and other equipment attached to it, it sinks. If it were a rowboat with no motor or equipment and you submerged this rowboat, it would still float but this is not about rowboats.

In the case of a typical fiberglass boat, since it is only about ½ inch thick on average, it sinks because it isn't thick enough to displace enough water. In the case of really big boats or ships they are usually made of steel and tend to sink even faster. Conventionally built boats or ships depend on one main factor to stay afloat. Don't let water get inside. A boat or ship built the way I am describing wouldn't be bothered too much if it ran into the rocks and tore a hole in the bottom. It would get lower in the water and the captain might be bothered but the boat would remain afloat. A boat or ship can be made of fiberglass or steel but it would need to be thick enough to displace enough water that weighed significantly more than the material itself. That is to say that the section of hull could have skins of fiberglass or steel or aluminum or whatever the boat designer preferred but separated by a lightweight core between the skins, so that, that section of hull, when immersed in water, displaced enough water that weighed more than the section itself and the proportionate amount of motor and equipment onboard.

Another way to think about it is a square bottle with the top on. This bottle will float because the sides are separated by air and therefore the entire volume of the bottle will displace enough water to allow it to float. If you take the top off the bottle and allow water to enter the bottle, only the sides of the bottle will displace water and since the sides are made of glass and the glass is heavier than water, it sinks. The core of the structure I describe is like the air in the bottle, it will not allow water to enter the space between the skins. It is somewhat lightweight, like air, but unlike air, it has qualities of strength that combine with the strength of the skins to form a structure where the strength of the entire unit is more than the sum of the strengths of the individual parts, much more.

Small boats can be made strong yet light by adding thickness to the hull in the form of lightweight cores that displace enough water to make them virtually unsinkable. A 20 foot boat would have for example a 2 inch thick hull, a 30 foot boat, a somewhat thicker hull and so on. A 500-foot ship may have a hull that is a foot or more thick. These figures are only to help you understand the idea that the bigger it is the thicker it needs to be. Calculations would need to be done for each size and type of boat or ship by the designers. Because of the much lighter weight of this kind of vessel, a hull style would be required that would allow it stability when standing still because it will not be very deep in the water. There are added benefits to this type of construction. Some of these are obvious such as less engine, fuel, etc!

A floodable keel would provide stability when not moving but would also allow the boat to "hunker down" in rough weather and provide counterbalance against "turnovers". By the use of inlet and outlet doors in the bow and stern this water weight can be removed as needed simply by accelerating the vessel and could also be used as a braking system by allowing water to enter while underway. A hull, which includes the use of properly designed stabilizers in the aft portion of the hull, would also provide some lift to get more of the hull out of the water when underway allowing for more efficient travel. This same design can be for both small and large boats or ships and has the advantage of a much shallower draft. Large ships would be able to enter ports previously denied them because of a much shallower draft and would certainly save money in fuel which is a major factor in shipping costs. When in really bad seas, with the keel chamber filled, the boat would be self-righting in the event of a turnover. Large ships carrying heavy cargoes could be made even thicker than would be normally required to make them float with a heavy cargo even if filled with water.

In the case of smaller boats that are trailered, built in retractable wheels to replace the trailer could be a very practical feature, as the lighter weight would allow it. You could put your boat in the water in one place and take it out at another place without worrying about having a trailer. Anyone who has dealt with a boat on a trailer knows what a pain in the you know what that can be. A further benefit is that you don't have to drag around all that extra weight and expense of a trailer.

A lighter boat takes less of a beating, uses less gas, needs less engine power for the same speeds and also means you could increase the range of the boat. In today's small boat market, the outboard motor usually cost's more than the boat does, so if you cut the weight by half, you save quite a bit of money just on the motor. Aside from the savings, there is one other factor that the boat manufacturers should consider. Many people do not like boats because they know that they can sink. If they knew they could safely venture out onto the water, many more would.

11

Aircraft

Safety has always been a large part of the thinking that goes into building and operating airplanes, however, along the way we slowly increased speed. Speed is the vital factor involved in safety or whether or not you could survive a mishap. Most aviation mishaps occur during landing or taking off and since landing and taking off speeds have increased dramatically, any mishap is inherently more dangerous today than the first days. I learned to fly in a piper cub and did so at only about 45 miles per hour while landing and taking off and I never had much fear because I figured I could always jump out when I was close to the ground if things didn't go as planned.

Today a typical landing or taking off speed for modern jets is 4 times that, so jumping off is no longer an option. The reason for these increased speeds is that the air flowing over the wings must go fast enough to create enough suction on top of the wings in order to lift the airplane and since airplanes got heavier and heavier more and more power was required to reach these higher landing and take off speeds. An airplane the size of a 747 that weighed ½ as much could still travel at 600 mph when it wanted too but would have the decided advantage of landing and taking off at roughly half the speed of the heavier one. Survival rates would follow suit in the event of a mishap due to the slower speeds..

As with the example used to reduce the weight of a car, the same principles apply to building airplanes. We can build airplanes today using composite sandwich panel principles with lightweight core materials. Aluminum can be used as the skin as it is used today except that the skin could be much thinner because it is supported throughout its entire surface by the lightweight core, in comparison to the aluminum skin in frame construction where it is only supported at those places where it is riveted to the ribs and stringers of the frame. Another advantage of sandwich construction is a two for one thing. In typical frame construction only the exterior skin is counted on for strength along with the frame itself. The inside is generally used more as a cosmetic feature than for strength. You wouldn't want to lean up against a rib or a stringer, while seated, so panels are added to the inside along with insulating materials to make things more comfortable. These things naturally add more weight but do not contribute significantly to the strength of the structure. By building the structure using the methods I am describing you get a two for one deal. An interior that you can lean on that also contributes to the strength not to mention the fact that the core has excellent insulation properties, so you could even say you get three for one. Naturally what follows, are smaller engines, less gas, lighter landing gear and so on but more importantly, slower takeoff and landing speeds. The slower you go, the more time you have to figure things out if things go wrong. Just like when you drive a car. Hitting something in a large airplane at 75 mph is a lot less demanding of the plane and its contents than hitting something at 150 mph, not to mention there would be much less fuel onboard.

I said earlier that I would question the weight compared to the use as I did with cars. A 4-engine jet weighs, let's say 330,000 lbs at takeoff. The airplane itself weighs 160,000 pounds, the passengers and baggage weigh 40,000 pounds and the fuel for a long flight would weigh 130,000 pounds, so we need 330,000 pounds to carry 40,000 pounds of payload. Not a very pretty picture is it? Cut the weight of this same size airplane in half to 80,000 pounds and you will need half the fuel for the same performance. You now have a total of 185,000 pounds versus 330,000 pounds for a 40,000 pound payload. If airplanes were lighter they could use more airports with shorter runways. We could then get to the airport faster than to our destination, which sometimes isn't possible in today's world. As for the actual construction of a lighter weight aircraft it would be accomplished by the use of adhesives and modern epoxies to attach the skins to the core material eliminating the need for the thousands or possibly millions of rivets and the many other parts such as ribs and stringers and interior panels needed in frame construction. This new type aircraft would require significantly less parts and again fewer parts which equal less work equals less cost, less pollution, etc! Sometimes this is referred to as the "KISS" method. Keep it simple, stupid. The best part of this way of building is the fact of lower speeds for take off and landing.

While transcribing the discussion on airplanes and why and how to reduce their weight from my handwritten notes into my computer, I became aware of the demise of the space shuttle Columbia and its brave crew, I had not intended to include space vehicles in this book as a subject because I didn't feel it related to things we use in our daily lives as we do regular aircraft and cars and such. We use the many wonderful by-products of our space program but not the vehicles themselves, at least not yet.

The time now is about 2 days after the accident and I have been watching with interest the many discussions on TV about this unfortunate tragedy. As is usual in this type of accident the focus goes to what happened to cause this and as of this writing it appears that a few heat shield tiles were damaged by insulation foam coming off the external fuel tank during takeoff and upon reentry some 16 days later were the reason for the failure of the ship. This was due to the super high temperatures and winds generated at reentry speeds of around 12,000 mph.

The many people involved with the space program and other experts that are on TV are saying, that we will get to the "root" cause of why it happened, so that whatever it was, could be fixed. The root cause will probably end up as tiles or the insulating material on the external tank and methods to improve on this will be implemented eventually. Looking at this objectively you could also say that heat is the root cause and then say that the reentry speed is the root cause because it was the speed that generated the heat. I would take it a step further and say that weight is the root cause of this sad event because there wasn't enough fuel left to slow the ship down on reentry. Maybe the real root cause is our handed down way of thinking.

The space shuttle weighs about 180,000 pounds and carries a payload of about 50,000 pounds An additional 4,250,000 (4 ¼ million) pounds are attached to the exterior of the shuttle in the form of fuel, fuel tank and detachable rocket motors. This is about the most dramatic example of inefficiency I could describe in an aircraft, or a spacecraft for that matter. The shuttle is at the same time, an aircraft and a spacecraft.

This same size structure can be built using lightweight cores and skins instead of the current frame method the shuttle uses which is similar to regular airplanes, consisting of ribs, stringers and spars etc! Various, graphite epoxies, carbon fibers, titanium, and other strong yet relatively light materials are presently being used but are used mostly for their properties of heat resistance, along with the 25,000 or so heat protection tiles and thermal blankets that are currently used on the shuttle. It is my opinion that the same size shuttle could be built at less than half the weight of the current shuttles by using a form of the lightweight core with exterior and interior structural skins this book talks about and still have the ability to carry the required payload to orbit. Many of these materials are available or even being used by NASA today. A case in point is where NASA reduced the weight of 42 crew storage lockers inside the shuttle by as much as 83% by the use of Kevlar/epoxy sandwich panels with a non-metallic lightweight core, replacing the original lockers made of aluminum.

A change in tactics by NASA would be required to also eliminate the millions of pounds of weight represented by the associated external tank, its fuel and booster rockets. A change in tactics means that instead of going straight up to overcome earth's gravity, which unfortunately precludes the use of Bernoulli's wonderful principle to overcome some of the gravity. A gradual increase in altitude could be used to take advantage of the fact that the shuttle is also an airplane which is presently not being taken advantage of by the shuttle on the assent portion of the trip. It only fly's like an airplane on the way back. Smaller and lighter rocket engines inside the shuttle could be used to take off using it as the aircraft it is. Sufficient fuel could be carried to reach space by gradually increasing speed as atmospheric drag decreases with altitude. If it were deemed necessary or desirable, additional and smaller detachable power could be used to assist during the initial lower atmospheric stage of flight where much of the fuel is depleted. Possibly, the same method used by NASA to carry the shuttle around the country by mounting it on top of a 747 could be used to carry it to 50,000 feet or so in order to save fuel on the way up similar to what we did with the old X-15, the first spacecraft.

The problem with going straight up is the 4 million or so pounds of fuel required for that approach. Most of that fuel and the rockets are used just to lift the fuel itself. Columbia did not encounter a friction heat problem on the takeoff because the speed while going thru the atmosphere on the way up was not fast enough to generate the same high heats and winds encountered during the descent phase. If the shuttle was light enough and had sufficient power and fuel on board to allow a gradual descent slowdown in space before and after hitting the atmosphere there would be no need for the various heat shields designed for temperatures of 3000 degrees. The various heat shield tiles, thermal blankets and associated cooling systems are a significant part of the shuttles overall weight. Speed could be adjusted to match the density of the atmosphere as the shuttle descends by the use of computers to stay within the operating limits of the craft and eliminate the need for non-structural heat resistant materials.

In other words instead of a "falling down" type reentry, a gradual slowing down type reentry, under power, could be used, starting in space and then reentry into our atmosphere at speeds where heat is not a problem. Instead of traveling at 12,000 mph when encountering the atmosphere, it could be at much lower speeds where heat just wasn't a factor. Once the vehicle reached speeds where it could again be operated as an aircraft rather than a spacecraft it could continue normally to a landing with power available if required instead of the one shot only landing it has to make today.

I have heard a NASA official state that such a method was against the "laws of physics", but that doesn't make sense. At least, not if the craft was light enough. During the descent stage it requires power, (thrust) to slow down just as you need power to go up. NASA could make these changes rather easily because they are well versed in lightweight sandwich panel construction and fully understand the benefits. What would be required of NASA is a new way of thinking about how to go about getting to space and back, a way that does not involve super high speeds in atmospheric flight where so much heat is generated. In order to accomplish this, they would have to change the way they build their craft. It is also possible that the weight of the payloads sent into space could be reduced somewhat using some of the techniques described here. A lighter shuttle going to space more like an aircraft would save enough money so that more flights could be made more often. If it were determined that insufficient fuel could be carried to fly up and back, then possibly other "tanker" flights could take payloads of fuel to the international space station for the use of other flights on their return voyage. Sort of like a gas station in the sky. It is pretty obvious to me that an organization like NASA with all their knowledge and experience could do these things if they wanted to, all they would need is to want to.

Of the thousands of comments made by people knowledgeable in space travel and the construction of these vehicles and the many comments on the internet written by regular folk, I have not encountered the word "weight" as a root cause and that is why I decided to add my 2 cents worth about the space business. I make no claims to knowledge of astrophysics other than some basic physics insight and some know-how in lightweight construction. As to whether or not this information will be useful in space travel depends on those in that business taking a closer unbiased look at the possibilities.

I personally, do not think we need to be in space other than to place the useful satellites in orbit around the earth that we all use. I feel we should leave exploring other planets until we more fully understand how to take care of our own.

12

Ocean Land

A number of years ago, I heard a commercial by a real estate company that said, "Buy land now because they don't make it anymore!" Well, in my simplistic way, I thought, Why not? How come they don't make it any more? What is land? Well of course, land is something you stand on and build on! If I can make a floor and stand on it, why can't I make land? Oh, I know, there isn't any space left. Then I thought, well why not build land on water? There's plenty of that around. If you build it light enough to float and build the structures on it in a similar fashion, it shouldn't be a problem. I mean, we stand on boats don't we? After considering this for a number of years, I came up with a basic form of "land" that could be built cheaper than you can buy regular land for.

Because of the strife between some peoples in many parts of the world, the location or the lack of land is the problem more so than the price. Many of the current problems in the world are the result of not enough land in certain areas. In some cases it is land that has historical value to the parties involved but since there does not seem to be an answer to these problems such as in the Mid-East, using the space available on the nearby water would be a sensible solution. This is space that is not in contention and is not being used by anyone. When you can provide space for building and living at an affordable price, you would be doing more than just making money or providing a neat place to live. By providing a few islands in the Mediterranean Sea or the Sea of Galilee for the Palestinians or the Israeli Settlers, things would cool down a bit. The same could be said for other hotspots in the world. An island about a mile in diameter could easily accommodate more than 4000 homes and businesses. I am sure that the Israelis and the Palestinians are spending much more money trying to maintain some sort of peace than it would cost to build some "sealand." Living on a mobile island is like living in an RV, you can always move the Island or even your part of the Island if you don't get along with your neighbors.

How can this be done, knowing that land needs to be rather big and stable? The best way would be to again copy nature, more specifically, bees. They build pretty large structures in relation to themselves by using one basic part, or shape, and that is a hexagon. A hexagon is nature's most efficient shape for joining parts to each other. In order to build this floating island, you would need to do it with parts that are maximum size yet still be able to be handled without the use of heavy machines. A hexagon about 10 feet in width and about 1 foot thick would be about right. This would allow each hexagon to support about 4400 pounds before it submerged, allowing for the weight of the foam and the cement coating it would need. Joining together just 100 of these hexagons would support half a million pounds. A sizable "Island" consisting of a few thousand of these modules will accommodate a small city that can be grown as needed. This type of material is not affected by water and since cement increases its strength in water, the two together are ideal for the job. They also happen to be the cheapest building materials available today.

The design of the basic "module" would use a simple attachment device so that as each module is produced, it can easily be attached to the one before it in the water. As for how to produce this system, a mold would allow each module to be completed with cement and attachment device when it comes out of the mold. After the fiber reinforced cement skin is allowed to cure, the module can be added to the ones before it in the water. When enough pieces are produced and attached to each other in the water, the entire production operation can be transferred to the new "land".

The stability of this new land would depend on how big the island is. To be a true island, capable of existing on the open seas, it would need to be about a third of a mile in diameter with a beach area around it about 200 feet deep. This would be sufficient to ward off any extra large waves keeping in mind that unlike regular seashore land, the outer perimeter of this type of "land" would be able to rise up and over incoming waves. The outer fringes of the island would need to be designed somewhat differently than the interior parts to allow for wave absorbing features. In protected waters such as lakes or inland seas, much of this beach area can be used for more housing or other structures. An island of 2000 feet or so in diameter would be so stable that you would think you were on land. This type of system, when being attached to existing land in a bay or other protected waters could be whatever size you like for few or many houses or other uses. Structures put on this new land would be built using the same methods of lightweight construction used to build the land itself. A hexagon makes an ideal part to build geodesic dome shaped houses and other buildings. Dome structures are easier to build, they are stronger and a dome shaped structure is the best shape for purposes of wind resistance. They are also more efficient in terms of space versus structure than typical box like structures. Please forgive me if I am going too fast for you to get your mind around the idea of building land. What I am describing here is very "low tech" and extremely doable.

There have been other attempts to build land on the seas but they failed. They never came to be mainly because of the enormous expense involved in their construction. One design I became familiar with a few years back anticipated using large steel interconnected floatation chambers. They were quite complicated and expensive to produce and therefore the idea never got off the ground, so to speak. In order for this new land is to be seaworthy, it has to be large and it must be completely unsinkable. The method and materials I am describing fulfill these requirements

The two basic materials involved, cement and EPS foam are both non-toxic and non-polluting and are at the same time, recyclable. They are also very available. EPS is an oil product but since it is so lightweight it requires very little oil to produce large volumes of the material. Besides, if some of these things come true, we will need something for the oil companies to do.

.There needs to be a complete infrastructure incorporated into the "island." To be entirely self contained it should have its own electrical generating systems. I say systems, plural, because there are various ways to produce energy at sea. One obvious method is to use the power of the movement of the tides and currents. Separate hexagonal "energy modules" allows for placement of relatively small water turbines, turned by the ever present moving water underneath the island. These would be rather simple water wheels attached to electrical generators that are turned by the moving currents. Individual "energy modules" would allow for placement at each house or facility that requires electricity, eliminating the need for a centralized power station or an electrical grid system.

The beauty of generating electricity on an island like this is the fact that if you can produce electricity in one place on the island, you can produce it anywhere on the island, separately or all at once because they all tap the same source. There is an additional source of energy that would be available to the island and that is called solar energy. Solar panels today have become much more efficient and cheaper and can be placed wherever required about the island and used in conjunction with other systems. Producing power at sea is inherently easier than on the old fashioned type of land. In the case of land being provided on enclosed bodies of water where currents did not run such as lakes or inland seas, existing land based energy stations could be connected to the new land to supplement the island's energy systems if required.

While on this subject of energy production, I will also mention that these same "energy modules" would have another method of producing electricity. On the bottom of each energy module would be the "water turbines" to drive the generator while on the top would be located a "wind turbine" that could be connected to the same generator to take advantage of another of natures helpers called wind. Theses natural sources of power, wind and water, can be used either separately or both can be used at the same time.

At times it may be more advantageous to use the wind than the water for energy. One of those times may be while underway as it may be that while underway the current runs in the same direction you are going. If I didn't mention it before, yes, the island would be able to move. What would be the use of such an island if one couldn't take advantage of going south in the winter and north in the summer? Of course it wouldn't move so fast that you would have to hold on to something. Something this big would travel in the neighborhood of 2 or 3 knots. It would take a while to get from say, the North Atlantic to the Caribbean but so what. You could sit in your backyard and have a barbeque or go out to a nice restaurant while you're getting there. Some may want to do a little fishing in their backyard to pass the time. All you would need to do is lift one module up or just make a hole in it. The idea of living on an island like this is that you're never really going somewhere when you're going somewhere, you're already there.

By now you probably wonder? How does something this big get "underway"? Just as there are redundant means of generating electricity, there would be various methods of propulsion depending on conditions at the time. If wind were available, which it would be most of the time, those same individual "windmills" which are used to turn the generators in each energy module would be designed to power the omni directional water turbines-cum-water paddles for propulsion. Naturally, any long distance travel would be planned to take advantage of natural ocean currents. It goes without saying that an anchoring system would be available when needed.

In today's world, Satellite navigation and meteorological information is readily available. Worldwide weather forecasting would provide ample time to avoid hurricanes. Computers would do most of the work in handling these systems. A third method that would be available to use for propulsion is the old fashioned one called sails. Retractable sails could be placed wherever and whenever it was felt they would be advantageous. Engines could be used also if it were deemed necessary. One thing to remember, on an island of this size, there is plenty of room for whatever you want or need. Also, weight is not a major consideration for something like an engine because as I mentioned before, each 10 foot module is capable of supporting over 4000 pounds. If necessary, any modules that were required to support more than that could simply be made thicker. A two foot thick module will support 8000 pounds. This is not a very complicated system. It can be modified wherever and whenever necessary, even after it is built. Just replace a few modules with whatever you like whenever you like. In the event of an island that wanted to stay in one location but may have to move occasionally, tug boats could be utilized thereby saving the cost of built in propulsion.

You could take out a few modules in your backyard to create a swimming pool and put them back in when you get tired of it or the water got too cold. A net could be fastened underneath the pool to keep people from straying too far from the pool or to keep unwanted underwater visitors out of the pool.

While we are on the subject of pools with a net, it is also a good way to have your own little fish farm. Creative waste management would provide food for the fish to grow along with whatever natural food there would be. There are similar net fish farms producing Tuna presently in operation in coastal waters of Australia. Some modules could be allowed to accumulate barnacles and other sea growth underneath to attract fish. All the other modules can be cleaned as needed just by lifting them out periodically one at a time. Other marine foods could be developed such as oysters, crabs and certain seaweeds that are edible and nutritious. There are people that could provide knowledge about this type of thing.

Hydroponics modules would be suitable for growing vegetables and fruits. Dirt could be used as a growing medium also but it would not be as efficient as hydroponically grown food. Even trees can be planted wherever you like. I am not talking about giant oak trees and such but smaller fruit trees and the like. Water can be provided by having a certain number of modules converted to evaporation stills using the seawater underneath to condense on plastic coverings thereby providing fresh water. Modules used for planting can be covered with transparent plastic domes that would act as evaporation stills and water the plants directly as well as be a protection for the crops from the elements as a sort of self watering hothouse. Each house could designate modules for whatever type food they would like to grow. You could have one for onions and lettuce and your neighbor could have tomatoes and green peas which could be traded or sold amongst other neighbors, cutting down on the need for distribution systems and warehousing.

This is not very high tech; it is just another way of doing things, things that have already been done and proven. Water for the use of the island can be produced by banks of these evaporation still modules along with small osmosis plants if necessary. Another back up system for water would of course be to have water tanks modules made from the same materials as the rest of the island that could be refilled by rainwater or whenever near shore or by supply ships. Of course the island would have its own built in port so that boats and ships could visit. Naturally the island would also have its own ferry service. Small airplanes could land on the island also. The inhabitants could give tours to cruise ship passengers who might want to come "ashore" to visit the restaurants or see a show in one of the island nightclubs. A few nice motels would be there if visitors wanted to spend the night.

Some of the inhabitants of this "island city" could specialize in different foods and a trade system developed such as two oysters for one fish or something like that, or just plain 50 cents each, whatever. After a while it may be that one island could trade goods that that island specializes in with another island that is set up for a different type of product because of where it spent most of its time or the people living on it suited that particular type of product. You could have an oyster island, a hydroponics lettuce island, a chicken island or a TV set island or even a cell phone producing island. The possibilities are endless. Once a year all the islands would get together somewhere and have a big trade fair. By that time, someone would probably figure out that they needed to enlarge the Panama or the Suez Canal to allow passage of all these islands. That shouldn't be a problem though because instead of enlarging the canal, the island itself can be made narrower by separating the island into smaller parts for the canal passage and then rejoining them on the other side.

By now you have probably noticed that I am not treating this island building idea as a fanciful subject. I feel that it will be the way human beings will have to go if we want to maintain our present population growth and the necessary shelters. Population growth is an exponential thing. The more people there are, the more babies there are, the more babies there are, and the more people there are. Learning to live on the other 70 percent of the world is the natural way for us to keep our world balanced and at the same time advance civilization. Airplanes and even cars were considered "fanciful" ideas before they got going.

I have read various stories of the fabled continent of "Atlantis" and the idea that their civilization dispersed to other parts of the world after their land disappeared. At that time the population of the world may have been such that it was advantageous to spread people around to the various continents.

The name, "Atlantis," in its root form, to me at least, means "to the land." By the same reasoning, the name "America," in its root form, means, "to the sea."

The letter "A" means "to" and "mer," means "sea." Maybe thousands or millions of years ago the Atlantians were fated to populate the land. Today, it is possible that we are supposed to populate the oceans. I know it seems a bit of a stretch for someone just learning about the idea of being able to live on the seas, but I thought I would mention it anyway. To further strengthen the case, "Amerigo" was the original name of America.

I do not know how a city island would operate in terms of laws or regulations because there would be no laws until the folks living on it decided how things should work. In a way it would be like starting your own country. Actually, not in a way, it would be starting your own country. It is possible that a company could build such an island and sell or rent the properties on it. If this country or another one wanted to expand they could do so by claiming the island as sovereign territory, similar to how they do with ships. Current international laws of the sea allow for new countries to be established as long as they are not on existing land or islands. These considerations would be up to those involved and is admittedly beyond my expertise and knowledge.

. Building and living on islands, may seem to be a farfetched and "outlandish" idea, but when considered, it makes a lot of sense if you take into account all the benefits. We have managed to get to the moon without any real purpose to do it and have overcome some very daunting technical challenges in doing so. We have spent untold billions of dollars and taxed many brains to figure out how to turn atoms into bombs. Neither of these endeavors has given us any real lasting improvements to the way we live our lives or for that matter helped the world in its operation. Yes, it's true we have enjoyed some spin off benefits from these enormous efforts such as atomic power plants and space developed gadgets. These advances would have happened in any case simply by letting science progress as it always has without spending all that money for a few rocks from the moon or for bombs to kill cities at a time.

This space available to us called seas and oceans are underused and we could be living comfortably on them. If done properly and with vision, it can be accomplished in a helpful and non-polluting way. We can learn to produce the energy we need without damaging our environment as we do now. Moving water currents, sunshine and wind are inexhaustible and limitless supplies of energy. Practically everything the inhabitants of this island could need, exists on or in the oceans. We can produce the water we need by removing the salt from the limitless supplies that would lay beneath our feet and simple sunshine would do the work. What I am talking about is not pie in the sky stuff. Growing food and even keeping livestock are more than possibilities, they are entirely doable. Island fish farms, done in the right way would even reduce the depletion of our natural fish stocks because we would be feeding them as they grow. We presently take fish from the sea without feeding them. Whatever wasn't produced on the island could be supplied by our non moving land based neighbors. Just as a city grows on regular land, floating islands can be grown as needed. All you have to do is add some more modules produced by the module plant already in existence on the island. In the case of Islands built close to shore, roads can be built to the island by the use of the same basic modules.

Transportation on such an island can be accomplished rather easily since distances are not very great meaning lightweight electric cars and other vehicles would be more than suitable. Everybody could have a boat if they wanted one as the island would have docks and water roads built in simply by not putting modules wherever you wanted a water road. If you wonder how this is possible without affecting the integrity of the island, it can be done by simple underwater connection ties to take the place of a module that wasn't there. As the island grew and things needed to be changed, moving roads or even houses can be easily accomplished by moving modules. There are really no limits to what can be done. Pretty much whatever you can think of can be built using some of the lightweight and simple methods described. We already have the technology and know-how to do whatever we want to. All we lack is to want to.

OK, so we can build these islands that allow us to live safely on the oceans of the world but what is it going to cost? Well, let's see, an island 2000 feet in diameter for example, has 3,170,000 square feet. Of that, 200 feet of the outer perimeter would be wave absorbing beach area, which would leave 2,028,800 square feet available for building and common area. First let's take a look at the cost of the basic 10 foot by 1 foot thick hexagon modules to make the whole island. We would need 34,870 modules for an island about a third of a mile in diameter. The perimeter modules will require a little less material than the inner area but for purpose of cost estimate I will count them the same. Because of the large amounts of EPS involved and the molding method that would be used to create these modules, it would be worthwhile to blow your own foam, that is, expand the basic poly-styrene in the mold. This is very similar to how they make a typical inexpensive Styrofoam ice cooler that you buy to keep your soda or beer cool when you go to the beach. Some little pellets are pre-expanded with steam and then put in a mold and with steam, expanded again and out pops the cooler. It is a very clean process and no gasses are emitted or pollutants put into the atmosphere. This same process would apply to the modules except that there would be a ½ inch layer of fiber reinforced lightweight cement sprayed on the inside of the mold first along with the placement of the attachment devices. After a few minutes of cure time the module is "popped out" and stacked ready for joining to the rest of the island. It sounds simple because it is. Of course to produce 34,870 modules you would probably need more than one mold, depending on how fast you want to build the island.

Based on current prices at a wholesale level, it would cost between $2 and $3 dollars a square foot to produce the modules including labor if you had about 10 molds set up in a production line fashion. It would take less than six months to build the island. If you wanted it to go faster you would need more molds. The majority of the work would be done by production machinery. Attachment devices, properly designed, would only take a few minutes to attach each one to the others already in the water. This whole process would take place in a bay or other protected water until it was big enough to take offshore. At this time you would already have some infrastructure installed and production would be taking place on the island itself. Based on these figures and needing about 35,000 modules the cost of the island itself without any houses or infrastructure would be about 15 million dollars. I have included the cost of the molds and production machinery such as cement and cement sprayers, conveyer belts, steam generators, etc! I then rounded off the number to keep it simple. So far we have, or better said need, about 15 million dollars.

Let's see about how many houses can comfortably fit on such an island. We have 2,028,800 square feet to work with when we deduct the 200 foot beach. Let's arbitrarily assign about 40% of this space to common areas for some streets, some business space, infrastructure and some administrative structures. That leaves us with 1,217,280 square feet of space for housing. Some of this space could be for condo type residences and some for detached homes. Some could be two stories and some one story. I cannot say how it would be, that would be up to professional city planners. For purposes of coming up with a figure to work with I will say that you can comfortably put 500 homes on this island. Some would be separate houses of various sizes and some could be condo type residences.

I understand the average price of a home in the United States is at about $200,000 dollars. It seems fair to me that a home on the water would command this average price, but let's just say $100,000 each in case the housing market drops by the time this island gets built. At $100,000 average each, this produces an income of $ 50,000,000 dollars. Deduct $15,000,000 dollars for the cost of the island itself and you have $35,000,000 dollars left. The homes and other structures will be constructed of the same type hexagons made from the same molds except that they don't have to be a foot thick whereas 6 inches thick will suffice. The molds can be adapted with separators to form triangles for the geodesic dome construction. It will cost only about $30,000 dollars per average house with about 1000 square feet of living space. The cost of about 20 mold "pops," which is enough to provide the basic dome parts for one house is about $5000 dollars; the rest of the $30,000 dollars is for the utilities, HVAC and labor to assemble and finish. Don't forget, the foundation and floor is already there, This would also include the energy module for each house which would cost about $3000 dollars each or less because there would be so many of them. We now need about $15,000,000 to produce the houses, so that leaves $20,000,000 dollars. Take out about $5,000,000 dollars for some infrastructure and you have a profit of $15,000,000 dollars. Not too shabby, considering much of the work is in producing the same part.

These numbers are only intended to show that the cost of building in this fashion is very low and that such a project could be a viable one. I haven't even included the profit from the building of business structures. Once production is set up on the island, there would be no reason why the island corporation or city state or whatever it would be called couldn't continue selling the houses for use by landlubbers. For that matter, once the island was established and in production, other islands or even land to attach to regular land could be produced and sold. I am sure there is a market, especially worldwide

Wrap up

This World is but one country and we are all citizens of that country. The boundary lines we have placed between nations cannot keep a citizen from the harmful effects caused by a fellow citizen in another nation. I have tried to create an awareness of what I see as existing problems as well as future problems with our world. The materialism that is the hallmark of our civilization needs to be tempered by spiritualism. I am not speaking about spiritualism in a religious sense; it is more in the sense that we are a small part of a perfect and wondrous universe, a universe that is beyond total human understanding.

Look up at the night sky and see that only a fool could think he could understand it all. It is this kind of spiritualism that we need, the belief that there is a plan, and that we are all the builders of that plan. We cannot afford to let our self importance continue changing the world as we do now. This planet that we occupy has a function as part of the larger whole and what we currently do does not fit the plan. The powers that be, the universe, just won't allow that to happen. It has seen other errors made in the past and has always acted to correct them. We are the only beings on this planet that have the power to think and reason, and because of our extraordinary powers, we have the slight advantage of seeing an unseen danger as it comes toward us. This edge gives us the opportunity to be able to take action and avoid that danger. We can see into the future if we use the powers given to us. This is why we were made masters of our world. We need to take care not to become the destroyers of our world. We can understand not only the how of our world, but the why, and with a little bit of foresight, we can understand the plan of the world. When we can do that, we can follow the plan and lighten up.

978-0-595-38035-0
0-595-38035-2